HIGHLY SUCCESSFUL PEOPLE

Prepare your Kids for Success! How to Increase your Influence and Raise a Boy, Break Free of the Overparenting Trap and Learn How Successful People Lead!

BY

Freddie Cress

TABLE OF CONTENTS

COPYRIGHTS   **21**

CHAPTER 1: INTRODUCTION   **25**

CHAPTER 2: 25 TIPS FOR RAISING A HEALTHY, SUCCESSFUL CHILD   **36**

   1. BECOME YOURSELF A HAPPY HUMAN   **37**

   2. AS MUCH WHEN YOU WOULD CELEBRATE WHEN A FAMILY   **38**

   3. CONSIDER YOUR MARRIAGE PRIORITY OVER YOUR CHILDREN   **39**

   4. GIVE UNDIVIDED ATTENTION TO YOUR CHILD   **39**

   5. SHARE MEALS WITH A PARTNER DAILY   **40**

   6. TEACH THE KIDS HOW TO CONTROL THEIR EMOTIONS   **40**

   7. LEARN TO MAKE MEANINGFUL TIES WITH YOUR CHILDREN   **41**

8. **PLACE FAIR LIMITS FOR YOUR KIDS** — 42

9. **MAKE SURE YOUR KIDS GET AMPLE SLEEP** — 43

10. **CONCENTRATE ON THE METHOD, NOT THE ULTIMATE OUTCOME** — 44

11. **GIVE UP TIME TO PLAY WITH YOUR CHILDREN** — 45

12. **REDUCE SCREEN TIME FOR YOUR KIDS** — 45

13. **ENCOURAGE THE CHILDREN TO KEEP A DIARY OF GRATITUDE** — 46

14. **LET YOUR CHILDREN KNOW FOR THEMSELVES** — 48

15. **SOLVE THE FAMILY PROBLEMS** — 49

16. **ENHANCE YOUR CHILDREN'S SERVICE AND KINDNESS** — 49

17. **ENCOURAGE A POSITIVE SELF IMAGE** — 50

18.	DON'T SCREAM AT THE KIDS	51
19.	LEARN YOUR CHILDREN TO FORGIVE	52
20.	LEARN TO THINK POSITIVE ABOUT YOUR CHILDREN	53
21.	BUILD A MESSAGE OF FAMILY PURPOSE	54
22.	FAMILY MEETINGS SHOULD BE ARRANGED REGULARLY	54
23.	ASK YOUR CHILDREN ABOUT YOUR FAMILY HISTORY	55
24.	ESTABLISH TRADITIONS FOR FAMILY	56
25.	SUPPORT THE KIDS FIND A MENTOR	57

CHAPTER 3: HOW SUCCESSFUL PEOPLE LEAD?   **60**

> ➢ **TIPS TO MAKE A YOUNG LEADER MORE EFFECTIVE**   **60**

- **TRUST, BUT BE CAREFUL NOT TO EQUATE CONFIDENCE WITH PRIDE** 61
- **MANAGEMENT'S VIEW** 61
- **INSPIRATIONAL ACTIONS** 62
- **BE POSITIVE, BUT DO NOT AFRAID OF TAKING CHANCES** 62
- **LET NOBODY SAY YOU THAT YOU CAN'T DO SOMETHING** 62
- **BE WELL THOUGHT-OUT** 63
- **FRUITFUL THOUGHTS** 63
- **YOU SHOULD SET YOUR GOALS AND STICK TO YOUR STRATEGY** 64
- **BROAD VISION** 64
- **KNOW YOUR VULNERABILITIES AND ABILITIES** 65
- **BE IMPARTIAL** 65
- **BE SMART** 66

- **BE ENTHUSIASTIC** 66
- **YOU'RE YOUNG, NOTE** 67
- **BONDING WITH OTHERS** 67
- **THINK BEFORE SPEAK** 67
- **GET A MAN (OR WOMAN) ON THE RIGHT** 68
- **KNOW HOW TO LISTEN TO SOMEONE AND HOW TO ONLY LISTEN TO YOURSELF** 68

CHAPTER 4: LOGIC BEHIND LEADING OF SUCCESSFUL PEOPLES 70

- **THEY ARE GEARED TOWARDS A TARGET** 72
- **THEY'RE POWERED BY PERFORMANCE** 72
- **THEY CONCENTRATE ON PRACTICE** 73
- **THEY'RE DIRECTED TO MEN** 74

- ➢ **THEY ARE WELL AWARE OF HYGIENE**   **75**
- ➢ **THEY ARE STRAIGHTFORWARD**   **76**
- ➢ **THEY ARE AUTONOMOUS**   **76**

CHAPTER 5: HOW SUCCESSFUL PEOPLE LEAD?   **79**

- ➢ **DEFINITE GOAL, DREAM, AND PURPOSE**   **80**
- ➢ **KNOWLEDGE AND QUALITY**   **81**
- ➢ **TARGETING**   **81**
- ➢ **STRONG AND CONSISTENT DISPOSITION**   **82**
- ➢ **VERSATILE**   **82**
- ➢ **EXPERT IN TIME MANAGEMENT**   **83**
- ➢ **STRONG COMMUNICATORS**   **84**
- ➢ **BOLD & BRAVE**   **84**
- ➢ **SUPPORTERS**   **85**

- **STRONG SELF-ESTEEM NATURE** 85
- **QUICK TO BEHAVE** 86
- **CONFIDENT** 87
- **GOOD READER** 87
- **INTUITION OF TRUST** 88
- **OPPORTUNITY TO LEARN AND WELCOME** 89
- **ACCEPTANCE OF ONESELF** 90
- **DREAM BIG** 90
- **GENERALLY ROUNDED AND EQUILIBRATED** 91
- **OUTSTANDING NETWORK** 92
- **FASCINATING** 92
- **RECOGNIZES FAULTS** 93
- **ABUNDANCE MENTALITY** 93
- **WELL PERFORMED CHARACTER** 94

- **GOOD COMPANY** 94
- **GOOD LISTENER** 96
- **SELF-CHECKING** 96
- **ALWAYS GET READY** 97
- **CHOICE** 97
- **CONNECTING TO YOURSELF** 97
- **AWARE OF CAPACITY** 98
- **START WITH A VISION** 99
- **CHAT REGULARLY AND SIMPLY** 100
- **DO NOT UNDERESTIMATE THE POSITIVE FORCE** 101
- **ENCOURAGE AND INSPIRE** 102
- **GREATLY WELCOME REVIEWS** 102
- **MANAGED BY EXAMPLE** 103
- **TAKE RESPONSIBILITY AND TAKE ACTION** 104

- **USING CONTROL TO SHIFT DRIVES** 104
- **GROW COMPOSURE** 105
- **NO 'SINGLE' MANAGEMENT STYLE EXISTS** 106

CHAPTER:6 HOW TO INCREASE AN INFLUENCE & RAISE AN ADULT 108

- **WHY BECOME AN ADULT CHILDREN'S ROLE MODEL?** 108
- **YOU SHOULD NEVER AVOID BEING A ROLE MODEL** 110
- **LET US CONTINUE WITH WHAT I THINK IS A FUNDAMENTAL TYPE OF SUCCESS FOR PARENTS** 111
- **MOST PARENTS ARE OBLIVIOUS TO THE VALUE OF THE QT BEFORE THEIR PUBERTY** 115
- **YOU SHOULD CONTINUE TO ASK QUESTIONS TO TEST YOUR**

- **CHILD'S HEALTH: HERE ARE QUESTIONS**   117
- ➢ **QT IS ALWAYS HARDER TO CUT OUT THAN SEEMS**   119
- ➢ **A FEW OF MY FAVORITE WORDS IS THAT YOU CAN'T BE A KID IF YOU WANT THEM**   119
- ➢ **WHY INTERACTION WITH ADULTS AFFECTS MOOD OF PARENTS?**   124
- ➢ **A MULTI-REACTION BAG**   125
- ➢ **THE PERFECT PLACES TO CATCH UP WITH**   126
- ➢ **GOOD CHATS HEAL NEGATIVE EXPERIENCES**   127
- ➢ **CONTINUOUS PRAYER**   128
- ➢ **SPEAK WITH RESERVATIONS**   128
- ➢ **BE A ROLE MODEL FOR THEM**   129

- ➢ **KNOW THAT YOU WERE YOUNG ONCE** 130
- ➢ **MAINTAIN THE DOOR OPEN** 131
- ➢ **MOVING THEM RATHER THAN YOUR OWN LIFE** 132
- ➢ **PROTECT THEIR HEART** 133

CHAPTER 7: WAYS TO RAISE AN ADULT 137

- ➢ **KEEP ON TOP OF IT** 140
- ➢ **ADMIRE THEM** 141
- ➢ **LET THEM OUTSIDE FOR FUN** 142
- ➢ **DO READ THEM CAREFULLY** 143
- ➢ **LET THEM PERFORM JOBS** 144
- ➢ **SUCCESS BECOME HAPPY** 145
- ➢ **FAMILY TIME SHOULD BE MAXIMUM** 146
- ➢ **FAMILY MEALS REGULARLY** 147

- **CELEBRATE LITTLE ACHIEVEMENTS** 147
- **PRUDENTLY SOLVES DISPUTES** 148
- **GIVE ATTENTION TO YOUR KID** 148
- **TEACH HOW TO MANAGE EMOTIONS** 149
- **SENSIBLY LIMIT YOUR CHILDREN** 150
- **GIVE TIME TO REST** 151
- **ARRANGE PLAY TIME FOR YOUR KID** 152
- **TV WATCHING TIME-LIMITED** 152
- **COURAGE YOUR CHILD TO READ** 153
- **NOT THE END JUST FOCUS ON MEANS** 154

- **ENCOURAGE FORMING NEW RELATIONSHIP** 154
- **YOUR KID WOULD BE ALTRUDIST** 155
- **TEACH THEM TO SERVE OTHERS** 156
- **YELLING IS PROHIBITED** 156
- **TEACH YOUR KID TO FORGIVE OTHERS** 157
- **PROMOTE POSITIVE THINKING** 158
- **ARRANGE GOOD CHILD MENTORS** 158
- **ACCEPT YOUR CHILD'S MISTAKES** 159
- **MOTIVATE THEM TO TRYING** 160
- **ALLOW THEM TO DO WHAT THEY WANT** 161

CHAPTER 8: HOW TO RAISE BOYS 165

- **THE CHILDHOOD OF THE BABY** 210
- **STOP STEREOTYPING SEXUALITY** 210
- **TELL YOUR BOY ABOUT BOUNDARIES** 212
- **SCHOOL GOING BOYS** 212
- **IMPEDE THE FEELING OF DOMINANCE** 212
- **ENCOURAGE THEIR EMOTIONS** 213
- **MIDDLE SCHOOL BOYS** 214
- **RAISE THEM TO MAKE HEALTHY INTERACTIONS** 214
- **DOCILE ACTIONS OF "TOUGH MAN"** 216
- **BOYS OF HIGH SCHOOL** 217
- **BE EXPRESS ABOUT ACCEPTANCE** 217

- **STAY CONNECTED** 218
- **COLLEGE GOING BOYS** 219
- **GIVE HELPING HAND TO THEM** 219
- **OPEN-TALKING** 220
- **PROVIDE HELP IN ANY SITUATION** 221
- **TEACH YOUR CHILD RESPONSIVENESS** 221
- **PLAY WITH YOUR BOY** 222
- **TELL HIM TO STUDY NOVELS** 223
- **ENHANCE HIS SELF-SENSE** 223
- **DON'T PROMOTE WRONG ACTIVITIES** 224
- **DO NOT MARK HIM** 224
- **TEACH TO RESPECT OTHERS** 225
- **SET RULES AND REGULATIONS** 225

- **SET A GOOD EXAMPLE FOR YOUR BOY** 226
- **SHOW YOUR LOVE AND AFFECTION** 226
- **SET A TIME TABLE** 227
- **FATHER'S RESPONSIBILITY** 227

CHAPTER 9: BREAK FREE OF THE OVERPARENTING TRAP & PREPARE KIDS FOR SUCCESS 231

- **CHILDREN WILL DISCOVER THE PLANET** 235
- **LEARNING WITH INNOVATIONS** 235
- **CHILDREN TODAY BENEFIT FROM OPTIMISM** 236
- **CHILDREN ARE OPPORTUNITY HUNTER** 237
- **CHILDREN SHOULD TAKE FILTHY JOBS** 238

- **SOCIAL SKILLS ARE MANDATORY** — 238
- **KIDS SHOULD HELP OTHERS** — 239

CHAPTER 10: WHAT WOULD YOU DO TO AVOID BEING OVER-PARENT? — 249

- **YOU'RE GOING THROUGH SMALL POWER STRUGGLES** — 252
- **YOU START TO MAKE YOUR CHILD'S PREFERENCES** — 252
- **YOU CAN NOT BEAR TO SEE THE LOSS OF YOUR CHILD** — 253
- **YOU'RE CONCERNED ABOUT OTHER PARENTS' ISSUES** — 254
- **YOU DISAGREE OVER HOW YOUR CHILD IS HANDLED WITH ADULTS** — 254
- **YOU ARE UNABLE TO RECOGNIZE ACCEPTABLE AGES** — 255

- **YOU DON'T OFFER MANY DUTIES TO YOUR CHILD**   256
- **YOUR BABY DRESSING**   257

CONCLUSION   259

COPYRIGHTS   261

COPYRIGHTS

© **Copyright 2020 By Freddie Cress**

- All rights reserved

This book

HOW TO RAISE HIGHLY SUCCESSFUL PEOPLE: Prepare your Kids for Success! How to Increase your Influence and Raise a Boy, Break Free of the Overparenting Trap and Learn How Successful People Lead!

By Freddie Cress

This document aims to provide precise and reliable details on this subject and the problem under discussion.

The product is marketed on the assumption that no officially approved bookkeeping or publishing house provides other available funds.

Where a legal or qualified guide is required, a person must have the right to participate in the field.

A statement of principle, which is a subcommittee of the American Bar Association, a committee of publishers and Association is approved. A copy, reproduction, or distribution of parts of this text, in electronic or written form, is not permitted.

The recording of this Document is strictly prohibited, and any retention of this text is only with the written permission of the publisher and all Liberties authorized.

The information provided here is correct and reliable, as any lack of attention or other means resulting from the misuse or use of the procedures, procedures, or instructions contained therein is the total, and absolute obligation of the user addressed.

The author is not obliged, directly or indirectly, to assume civil or civil liability for any restoration, damage, or loss resulting from the data collected here. The respective authors retain all copyrights not kept by the publisher.

The information contained herein is solely and universally available for information purposes. The data is presented without a warranty or promise of any kind.

The trademarks used are without approval, and the patent is issued without the trademark owner's permission or protection.

The logos and labels in this book are the property of the owners themselves and are not associated with this text.

CHAPTER 1: INTRODUCTION

Parenting specialists report on crucial facets of child-rearing, such as sleep, health, attachment, or training, but their guidance is usually narrow and prescriptive. We just do not need minimal knowledge as crucial as that about care and feeding for babies. What we need to learn more about how our children will be as successful as adults. We must also confront significant cultural changes in recent years — especially changes in technology and how these changes influence the relationship between our parents. How will the era of robotics and artificial intelligence work for our children? How's the digital revolution going to prosper? Parents globally know these anxieties.

As a young adult, I have taken some little advice, but I have chosen to trust myself for the most part. Maybe I was educated as a journalist or distrustful of my childhood authorities, but I was eager to discover the facts alone. I had my ideas about what children wanted, and I stuck to them, regardless of what other people think. In the minds of others, the outcome was, at best odd or strange. As if they were adults from day one, I talked to my girls. Naturally, most mothers turn to babies — a louder, more direct word speech. I don't. I trusted and confided in them. I never put them at risk, but neither did I stand in their way of life or taking the measured chance.

My philosophy was that I was trying to teach as soon as I could early in the first five years of zero to five. Above all, I wanted them to become confident children and driven, responsible people. I figured that they should face few problems because they could think about themselves and make rational decisions themselves. At the time, I had no idea that work would validate my choices. I pursued my intestines and principles, and I saw what served as an instructor in the classroom.

It's pretty strange to be a "popular" parent who has a magazine cover for your kids. I'm not aware of all the blame for their adult achievements, but all three were competent, loving, and willing men.

DETERMINATION, COOPERATION, AND COMPASSION

TRUST

We're in a worldwide crisis of faith. Parents are scared, and that frightens our kids – being who it is, taking chances, battling inequality. Confidence must begin with us. If we trust our parents, so we will expect our children to bring necessary and appropriate actions for empowerment and freedom.

RESPECT

Our children's sovereignty and independence are the most significant values we should give. It's our parental duty to cultivate the gift, no matter what it might be. Respect is a blessing, and it's a contribution to the community. It is the exact reverse to asking children who they should be, what profession they should be, and what their futures should look like.

INDEPENDENCE

Independence is based on a strong trust and respect foundation. Kids who learn to control themselves and to be accountable early in their lives are far more suited to face the struggles of their adulthood. Honestly, independent children can deal with challenges, failures, and boredom, all facets of life inevitable. And if things around you are in turmoil, you stay in control.

COOPERATION

Living together includes work as a family, at a school, or a job. Parents are expected to have their children engage in discussions, choices, and even discipline. When rule-following was one of the best talents in the 20th century, parents were tightly supervised. Dictating doesn't work much in the 21st century. Our children should not be asked what to do; instead, we will ask for their suggestions, work together, and find answers.

COMPASSION

It is odd but real that we prefer to treat people who are nearest to us without the courtesy and compassion that we give to others. Parents love their children, but they are so familiar with them, they still take pure goodness for granted. Yet, as a rule for the entire universe, they do not always know model goodness. Genuine compassion means appreciation and healing, loyalty to others, and an external view of the environment. It is essential to teach our children that the best and most exciting thing you can do is to better the life of someone else.

Our main aim is to build responsible individuals in an automated environment. That is what we do as parents, teachers, and managers — not only train children and run classrooms and management boardrooms but also lay the foundation for humanity's future. We grow human consciousness, and we do so more rapidly than ever before. You become your child's parent, and your child is the very being they become supposed to be with your faith and respect.

Within their babies, parents may create interest using similar approaches. They don't necessarily have to have the correct answers, but we do empower children to seek the right questions. We may say, "Let's find out if we don't know the solution. My grandson Noah often talks about the stars, planets, and the universe around him, complicated questions like "What are black holes? Do some work on Google, and we can go from there?" "And what does sound barrier mean? What does that mean?

How we are creating, whether we encourage creativity, is the imagination of a child. That takes me to the vision, a magnificently autonomous, curious by-product. Regrettably, our children are struggling when it comes to creativity and invention. In a report, a method was used to assess imagination and creative thinking in young children, based on NASA's innovation cycle. At age 5, 98% of children had a gift in creativity.

Nevertheless, at ten years of age, only 30% of children come in. Do you want to say how many people have retained their critical reasoning capabilities across our school system? It's just 2%.

You should do that as a mom, even if the imagination of your child isn't promoted in school: I used to place all kinds of furniture on a kitchen table for my girls. The posters, the colored paper, the books, Play-Doh, braiding yarn, and other handicrafts were given. They had to do what they wanted when they came home from college. I was also hunting for toys that could be assembled and built by them. The YouTube Kids App has interactive videos to make you learn about some sort of innovative idea.

Works such as these allow children to visualize and explore and, above all, play. Creativity comes from a sense of nature, and the child should be taught as one of the most specific items. A hint here: let it be. Without any help from you, they build their fantasy worlds. Think of a kid on the beach and all his fun games and adventures — collect cockroaches and shells, build sandcastles, skip bricks, jump on the waves. This activity makes them happy (and develops the right competencies).

CHAPTER 2: 25 TIPS FOR RAISING A HEALTHY, SUCCESSFUL CHILD

The growing parent would like to raise healthy and productive babies.

Yet out there are so many parental tips.

What do you listen to them? When should you attend?

So what advice is reliable?

I have read hundreds of academic articles and research journals to address these questions.

A collection has been compiled of 25 scientific aspects in which children are trustworthy and well adjusted.

1. BECOME YOURSELF A HAPPY HUMAN

As explained in Raising Happiness, emotional issues in parents are linked with psychological problems in their children. Not just that, but even less successful parents are frustrated people.

When your parents gave you one wish, what will it be?

Their response?

It wasn't because they were spending more time with their friends. Nor was it that fewer would nag their parents at them, or allow them more independence. The wish of the children was to have their parents less stressed and tired.

2. AS MUCH WHEN YOU WOULD CELEBRATE WHEN A FAMILY

Happy families enjoy the things significant as well as small: a busy weekend, a strong education, the first school day, a celebration of work, holidays, and birthdays. The parties can be as easy as walking together to the park, or as complicated as a surprise party. Happy families contribute to more comfortable kids, so rejoice much as a family.

3. CONSIDER YOUR MARRIAGE PRIORITY OVER YOUR CHILDREN

Child-centered families have anxious, tired parents and demanding babies. Today, our parents are too strong for our children to risk their lives and marriages.

"A complete marriage is the best gift that you can give to your children."

4. GIVE UNDIVIDED ATTENTION TO YOUR CHILD

When you want your children to be healthy and productive, it is essential to communicate well with them. One compelling way to do so is when talking to you and give them your full attention. It is to lay down the newspapers and computer gadgets and listen to what they say. You will respond more cautiously, enabling the children to be more communicative.

5. SHARE MEALS WITH A PARTNER DAILY

In almost every region, children who frequently eat with their families will thrive.

These children have more significant language, greater flexibility, and higher grades. They are less inclined to alcohol, smoking, taking drugs, or psychology. And this is because these families always feed together!

6. TEACH THE KIDS HOW TO CONTROL THEIR EMOTIONS

Kids who can help control their feelings rely on results. That is crucial. Some kids are much stronger visually.

- You should express yourself.
- Sympathize with your children.
- Explain to your children that all thoughts are appropriate, but not all behaviors.
- Recognize the success of your children. Your children should be encouraged. To help your children control their emotions.

7. LEARN TO MAKE MEANINGFUL TIES WITH YOUR CHILDREN

For childhood development and psychological well-being, maintaining good relationships is essential. Kids who do not have such interactions fare worse at school are more likely to have law issues and medical disorders. How do parents do to promote positive relationships with their children?

Parents should adequately respond to the emotional signals of their children (see point 6). Your children would feel better by doing so. This action is the foundation of self-esteem. Parents should build a bonding atmosphere for their children as well as show them how to settle conflicts.

8. PLACE FAIR LIMITS FOR YOUR KIDS

Parents who set and implement realistic limits raise children with trust and achievement. Explain to their children the logic of the rules. These people set the values behind the rules that are set by these people. They develop a closer relationship with their children, in which they become more trusting Families who don't set limits: "children take the absence of laws as an indication they do not care for their welfare, and their families don't want this task of becoming a mom." Yet children require limitations to take advantage of their abilities.

9. MAKE SURE YOUR KIDS GET AMPLE SLEEP

Evidence suggests that kids who are sleeping have:

1] Reduced brain functions

2] Can't concentrate well

3] are more likely to get obese

4] are less imaginative

5] Can't control their emotions

Set up regular dormitories and that distracting behavior after dinner to help your child get enough sleep. Often, don't require screen time for 1-2 hours after bedtime. Blue light from electrical devices changes the rhythms of sleep and hinders the development of melatonin. To enhance sleep efficiency, you should keep your kids' sleep as calm and as dark as possible.

10. CONCENTRATE ON THE METHOD, NOT THE ULTIMATE OUTCOME

Parents who over-accentuate success are more likely to raise children with developmental issues and unsafe behavior.

The way to concentrate on performance? Concentrate on this cycle. Children who are based – not on the expected result – on commitment and disposition wind up getting more results in the long run. See if you can appreciate the actual conduct, disposition, and commitment of your children. Naturally, they can produce better outcomes as time goes on.

11. GIVE UP TIME TO PLAY WITH YOUR CHILDREN

I don't mean arcade or iPad games when I say "play." I'm dreaming, ideally outside, about unstructured playtime. For children's learning and development, how playtime is essential. The study indicates that the less unstructured children are, the more likely it is for their physical, cognitive, financial, and behavioral well-being to develop problems. A playful disposition is also related to higher academic achievement. Offer your children more unstructured time for playing, and they can develop.

12. REDUCE SCREEN TIME FOR YOUR KIDS

The research cited to suggest a clear correlation between decreased satisfaction and less desire for Television. Good people watch less TV than sad people, in other words. A survey of over four thousand teens showed that those who had more TV would be more discouraged. For more TV exposure, this likelihood decreases.

Set an example by restricting your TV time for your son. You should also hold a private chat on the TV rules for your children.

(The study I found concentrated on Television, but with other screen time, I am confident the findings will still be similar.)

13. ENCOURAGE THE CHILDREN TO KEEP A DIARY OF GRATITUDE

Maintaining a journal of appreciation will increase your gladness by 25% in just ten weeks.

I'm sure if the analysis lasted longer, the findings will be much more remarkable!

They had more optimism for the future, and they got ill less often. Not only were the people who had a happy, grateful report.

How do you continue to build a journal of gratitude?

Phase 1: Grab your notebook and a pen and put it on a table.

Stage 2: Write down two or three things you're grateful for every night before you go to sleep. (These issues are not concerned about how 'large' or 'small';

Here are a few samples of what could be written:

- Beautiful sunset
- Caring family
- Marvelous chicken stew for dinner
- Food traffic on your way home

14. LET YOUR CHILDREN KNOW FOR THEMSELVES

The advantages of helping children organize their plans and set a report established their targets. For a fact, these children will be more diligent and concentrated and make better decisions. The study has observed that encouraging their children to pick their punishments is beneficial to parents. Children who do so often frequently violate the rules. Enable your children, as much as possible, to choose their activities. Twenty-four percent more often are students who take part in formal education because they want to go to kindergarten. Allow them the ability to make more decisions of their own as their children are older. As a result, they will be healthier and happier.

15. SOLVE THE FAMILY PROBLEMS

Kids with extreme family conflict are more likely to have poor school outcomes, substance, and alcohol addiction, and mental difficulties, as Kelly Musick revealed in this report. There are no surprises. I still connect with other parents through my job with children. I'm surprised by the number of families with big ongoing marriage problems among parents. This thing undoubtedly affects youngsters, who are less inspired, responsible, and dedicated. (Because of my findings, I believe that 30% of these relationships are split.)

16. ENHANCE YOUR CHILDREN'S SERVICE AND KINDNESS

Kids who feel like something about their life are happy too. What makes them more attractive in their lives? When it affects other people, it affects their friends and families, for example, in the group even charitable, children are happier if they offer treatments to others than if they earn treatments. Ironically, kids are better if they provide benefits that they have instead of the same procedures that they don't have. To inspire your children, as a family, to support others and be charitable.

17. ENCOURAGE A POSITIVE SELF IMAGE

The competent body image, although it can also affect boys, is particularly relevant for girls. One-third of 13-year-old girls are disturbed by their weight according to a survey undertaken by the Institute of Child Education. Furthermore, the Dove study has found that 69% of mothers speak against their children on their bodies. It influences the body's confidence in your children.

Anyways, in which the children should encourage a positive body image:

- Focus on the health effects of exercising and no more the impact it has on your looks.
- Focus more on the growth of your children's character and skills and less on their looks.
- For your children to exercising together as a family.
- Talk to your children about the media influences our view of our bodies.

18. DON'T SCREAM AT THE KIDS

When your kids yell, your home will become a permanent battlefield quickly. Under such a violent climate, children continue to feel confused and nervous. Put yourself away from the situation as you are going to lose your patience. Take 10 minutes before talking to your child again to gather your thoughts, and using "emotion therapy," to empathize with your children's emotions. When it works, visualize a boss or partner in a room with you. And you're going to talk to the kids more softly.

19. LEARN YOUR CHILDREN TO FORGIVE

Forgiveness is an essential factor contributing to children's happiness. Mercilessness was also related to fear and depression. Kids who learn to forgive will create good thoughts towards the past. It increases your joy and your pleasure with your work. Have the children's role models. Don't condemn those who wrong you and take the opportunity to solve personal disputes. Speak to your children about the value of redemption, so that it is a habit.

20. LEARN TO THINK POSITIVE ABOUT YOUR CHILDREN

Entirely positive children seem to be healthier. How do you instill constructive thought for your kids? It is one way to motivate them to keep a log of thanks. Any other forms are described here:

- Take a healthy disposition,
- Don't whine,
- Don't argue,
- Don't make a big deal out about spilled drinks, split platelets, and so on.
- See what goes better for everyone and embrace it,
- Take your children into the optimistic expression, e.g., "I like playing David

and Sarah" instead of "I hate to play for Tom."

21. BUILD A MESSAGE OF FAMILY PURPOSE

Any company, including your family, will have a mission statement. This thing is an outstanding step-by-step guide to develop a mission statement for your children. My own family did this – it was an essential operation!

22. FAMILY MEETINGS SHOULD BE ARRANGED REGULARLY

A 20-minute family lunch once a week would be suggested. During this conference, you posed these three questions to all family members:

1) What were your achievements over the last week?

2) Last week, what didn't you do so well?

3) In the next week, what are you going to focus on them?

My father held frequent gatherings when I was younger. Such collections brought together the family and reinforced the importance of connections between families. I still remember how nervous I was at these meetings to this day. So, if you haven't already, I urge you to begin this exercise.

23. ASK YOUR CHILDREN ABOUT YOUR FAMILY HISTORY

Evidence shows that children who have a better sense of self-esteem than children who care about their family backgrounds. This behavior leads later in their life to their success and satisfaction.

"Did you remember any of your parents' diseases and accidents when they were younger? "And did you remember those issues that come to your mother or dad in school?". Sharing the past of your family reinforces family ties and makes your children more resilient.

24. ESTABLISH TRADITIONS FOR FAMILY

Family traditions allow children to learn socially and to enhance family relations. Seek to build those traditions in your family with a conscience.

Several instances are as follows:

- Have breakfast every Saturday as a family
- Have a family boards game at evening games
- Cook dinner as a family
- Go for a walk at night

- Hold a weekly family meeting (see point 22)

25. SUPPORT THE KIDS FIND A MENTOR

Kids who have a trustworthy person in their lives are 30 percent healthier than children who don't have a reliable relative.

WHY ARE RELATIONSHIPS BETWEEN YOUNG PEOPLE AND ADULTS IMPORTANT?

Many adults don't know how to work with teens and young adults efficiently and authentically, nor do they have clear experiences from the youth. Although adults can be moral, young people also report being disregarded or underutilized or worse. If young people contribute substantially to the strategy and execution of a meeting or conference, it will be of value to both ensuring that adults do not talk on behalf of young people. Adults and young people are significant assets of a country. It's a great responsibility for parents to grow their children in such a way that they will be able to do innovative things in the future. This responsibility is not only for themselves but also for their country. Young people need great attention from their parents. Adults have a mind with a bundle of thoughts and views. They seek guidance to draw their imaginative pictures onto a canvass. This thing only happens with the help of parents.

Sometimes adults become worse in their actions and make decisions. They are unable to make decisions on their own. At that time, they are dependent on their parents. And parents have to be very responsible in this case.

CHAPTER 3: HOW SUCCESSFUL PEOPLE LEAD?

TIPS TO MAKE A YOUNG LEADER MORE EFFECTIVE

The core of this article is the personal experiences that I have in the form of advice as a young leader. It is for someone who wishes to become a seasoned chief or a senior one. I also have tips from close friends, leaders of their region.

TRUST, BUT BE CAREFUL NOT TO EQUATE CONFIDENCE WITH PRIDE

You will know what you are thinking about doing so. Speak with confidence as you talk.

MANAGEMENT'S VIEW

It's about offering something fresh or initial perspectives. Someone who knows and interprets life himself will separate himself from others. It means that you don't want anything off yourself. Try a specific description or interpretation also. You can never rely upon other expertise, job, or judgment to obtain that emotional distance and understanding.

INSPIRATIONAL ACTIONS

"Tell people to respond by demonstrating their determination and devotion to a better future. Make it easy if people want to support and join forces.

BE POSITIVE, BUT DO NOT AFRAID OF TAKING CHANCES

Is not afraid of being idealistic. If you lose, you must consider and change your abilities and weaknesses in the future. You will only optimize your ability by understanding your limit. Naturally, the breadth of the capacity will diminish with practice over time.

LET NOBODY SAY YOU THAT YOU CAN'T DO SOMETHING

If there's nothing, go and build it. Don't allow anyone to underestimate you in any situation. Usually, people never bear the success of others. They always find a way to let you down in any circumstances. This is the time to show your power and to accept challenges.

BE WELL THOUGHT-OUT

You will need to be coordinated to function efficiently. You seem to miss those things if you're disorganized.

FRUITFUL THOUGHTS

Capable of entirely and accurately articulating your feelings and speech (i.e., communication abilities). It also ensures that you can assign responsibilities and express your goals.

YOU SHOULD SET YOUR GOALS AND STICK TO YOUR STRATEGY

"The easiest way to lead is often scheduled, schedules, and strategies. Usually, the flow is more powerful, take it as it comes, and pursue any new opportunity. Nonetheless, your goal will still keep in mind your final game.

"See for your reasons, patient. Go on the path of yourself.

BROAD VISION

Be sure you solve an issue with your programs, campaigns, and attempts and have explicitly established what the problem is and how it is to be addressed.

KNOW YOUR VULNERABILITIES AND ABILITIES

Having a leader does not necessarily mean you are the brightest or most competent person at a party. It just means that you should coordinate people and use the abilities of each person. "The job of leadership is not straightforward — not everyone should. I believe you are not only a good leader, but there is no limit to what you will achieve if you are genuinely excited about your business. You can't slow down something important, and only your enthusiasm will move you.

BE IMPARTIAL

You have to be honest to win trust and admiration for your supporters. Do not look to your close friends or colleagues immediately if an opening occurs. Let us know and get the same opportunity, and everyone knows.

BE SMART

Seek an alternate approach if it doesn't work. If you don't have ample money, see how it can be quickly donated and loaned to you in your neighborhood. Be active and smart in any situation. Don't underestimate yourself and your capabilities. Believe in yourself more than others.

BE ENTHUSIASTIC

After all, hope is essential to improve the dynamics of this planet. "There appears to be what you think."

YOU'RE YOUNG, NOTE

Be robust! Be vigorous! I'm always trying not to be too bad. Recognize that you are still young and accept all the prime has to bring.

BONDING WITH OTHERS

You're never going to know if a human is useful. Via my family and peers, I built a support network. Everyone has an extensive network. If you want to communicate with a person you don't know, just enter and add a message.

THINK BEFORE SPEAK

Know when to talk, and when appropriate, give it. When a volunteer member of the team takes a mission or has a purpose assigned to him or her, they are committed to carrying it out. There are many valid explanations of why a person does not perform his / her duties, and if they do, you will embrace them. If I already have explained my goals or the inability to complete a mission (or have) affected the whole squad, I would not hesitate to be honest with everyone.

GET A MAN (OR WOMAN) ON THE RIGHT

It's a trustworthy guy. Surround yourself with the people who are credible and can work with them. Don't trust blindly on anyone. This habit sometimes leads to a significant loss.

KNOW HOW TO LISTEN TO SOMEONE AND HOW TO ONLY LISTEN TO YOURSELF

Try to prioritize yourself first. Listen to your heart. Develop the convincing power. It doesn't mean to listen to others. You must have to examine all the scenarios and circumstances and then pick a plan for a strategy.

CHAPTER 4: LOGIC BEHIND LEADING OF SUCCESSFUL PEOPLES

Many people question how they can excel and not know that they keep in them what they need to achieve their desired results. Productive people are today because of their customs. Behaviors at 95 percent dictate a person's conduct. Everything you are now and what you ever will be able to do depends on the consistency of your routines. You, too, can achieve happiness and lead a happier life by developing healthy habits and practicing positive behavior.

These seven effective ways of living are strong predictors.

The habits of successful people are:

- They are geared towards a target.
- They're powered by performance.
- They concentrate on practice.
- They're directed to men.
- They are well aware of hygiene.
- They are straightforward.
- They are autonomous.

For thousands of years, brilliant thinkers and theorists have been researching the quality of human life. For more than 30 years, I've been researching the subject myself. What I noticed was that the best people have healthy routines.

I've established seven helpful routines to build if you want to follow all you do to the fullest.

THEY ARE GEARED TOWARDS A TARGET

The first habit is to concentrate on the target. You ought to give yourself the typical target and to carry out simple, written priorities, creating everyday routines every day of life. The objectives are highly focused on these productive individuals. You know what you want, you write it down, you have outlined plans to fulfill that, and you revisit and reflect on your intentions every day.

THEY'RE POWERED BY PERFORMANCE

The second habit of productive individuals guides results.

This guide consists of two processes.

1) The first thing is to practice so that what you do is more comfortable.

2) Time control is the second method. This method ensures that you have particular goals on what you are doing and only concentrate on the most valuable use of your resources. Someone very successful is incredibly successful.

THEY CONCENTRATE ON PRACTICE

The 3rd significant practice you will build is constant operation. That is the most critical practice for material achievement. It's the desire to start to finish the job efficiently. You are capable of creating and sustaining a sense of urgency and a passion for action. Quick speed is essential about your success, whatever you do. You must resolve the delay, remove your doubts, and continue 100% for the accomplishment of your main aims. The blend of goal orientation, result orientation, and intervention orientation would guarantee almost complete results of themselves.

THEY'RE DIRECTED TO MEN

The fourth pattern is the attitude towards men. You place relationships at the core of your life. This habit is your opportunity to practice tolerance, empathy, sensitivity, and understanding within yourself. Virtually everything about your life's success comes from the desire to get along with others. The good news is that, as you agree, you will become a wonderful person in your ties with others.

As Aristotle said, it is only by doing it daily that you can develop every behavior. The more in your interactions with people you practice being a perfect guy, the more you internalize these characteristics and eventually become that guy.

THEY ARE WELL AWARE OF HYGIENE

Health literacy is the fifth habit of extremely productive individuals. You would also keep an eye on your food and eat only the correct portion all the time. You will continuously workout, using every muscle and joint in your body continues to keep the body relaxed and fit. And finally, you need proper rest and leisure habits that help you to live your years in good condition in combination with diet and fitness. Note, your wellbeing is the only thing you have and is entirely dependent on the behaviors you build in terms of your way of life.

THEY ARE STRAIGHTFORWARD

Honesty is the sixth behavior. In the end, the character you create as you live is more relevant than almost anything.

Sincerity means that with everything you do, you follow the 'principle of truth.' To yourself and the world surrounding you, you are utterly impartial. You give yourself straightforward values and align yourself around your beliefs. You create your dream and then live your life in line with the highest ideals. For anyone or something, you never sacrifice your dignity or your peace of mind. This honest attitude is essential for your enjoyment of all your other good habits.

THEY ARE AUTONOMOUS

The seventh discipline, and that of self-discipline, is the only habit that assures others. The most valuable single attribute you will build as a human is your ability to discipline yourself, master yourself, and control yourself. The nature of self-discipline correlates with progress in every area of life. All these behaviors can be formed as priorities, outcomes, response, people-focused, people mindful of safety, truthful, and self-disciplined. Regardless of your habits, you are who and wherever you are doing. Since the time of your childhood, your patterns developed mainly by mistake.

Today, by making the decision right now to decide the pattern, you can fully influence how you develop your attitude and character and anything that happens to you in the future. So, you'll experience success together as you build the same healthy habits that other successful people do. Your life is going to be infinite.

CHAPTER 5: HOW SUCCESSFUL PEOPLE LEAD?

You ought to be a follower of those who their dreams if you want to fulfill the goals of your life and to be incredibly popular. The more values that you possess, the more likely you are to excel. Successful people lead by setting some targets in their lives. Such people are very determined and punctual in their whole life. They set some rules to excel in life. Such people are the real heroes of the country.

HERE ARE SOME CRUCIAL POINTS; EVERY SUCCESSFUL MAN FOLLOWS:

DEFINITE GOAL, DREAM, AND PURPOSE
Successful people are still searching for meaning in general. You know what you want, and you have a vision about yourself. Ambiguous wishes and assumptions tend to unclear outcomes. This sense of purpose gives you the ability to stick to your goals and achieve your dreams.

KNOWLEDGE AND QUALITY

They are the best in their profession, irrespective of what they do. No research is too limited, and productive people are aiming for perfection. We are improving themselves and know that wealth is a by-product of their interest.

TARGETING

Successful people know how to work. You know that you can't do it all, so you concentrate on the activities which offer you the highest return on your goals. You don't believe in the multi-tasking myth, so you know the fastest way to finish your job is by completing something.

STRONG AND CONSISTENT DISPOSITION

Unique people have rational hope. Realistic as they behave and hopeful, as they think their success is imminent no matter what the outcome might be. They say they will take steps first, like a kid who is learning to walk, and then change their behaviors according to their input. This optimistic outlook helps them, if things are not done, to persevere and to be resilient.

VERSATILE

One misconception of the ordinary people is why they remain the course, regardless of what. This thing is only accurate if the purpose is still valid. Most influential individuals have done something different than what they wanted to do (Example: Steve Jobs started with machines, went to the animation, and made his comeback with the iPod). The future needs to evolve, and they learn even better today than before they began. It makes sense. Reasonable people know that there is no sense in continuing if their motives for doing what they are doing change.

EXPERT IN TIME MANAGEMENT

Successful people excel because they have learned a great deal. The best option is to make the most of the 24 hours available to us all. Extraordinary people respect their time and see the clear connection between the time and money they spend. Typically, the people who work with them are always on time and prepare to fulfill their deadlines by requesting rigorous schedules for their meetings.

STRONG COMMUNICATORS

People who can easily communicate are exceptional in their lives. Good communicators understand that it doesn't mean they know each other only because people speak English (or their dominant language). That makes them successful is that they are transparent and receptive to their interaction outcomes and that they are agile to obtain findings of their contact methods. They are experts in the creation of partnerships and differentiate what is said from what is not mentioned.

BOLD & BRAVE

We've always heard the phrase, "No risk. No reward." but how many of us take the risk required to get the reward we want? Not many, but for those who do, they are the ones who make it and become famous. The good are bold to start AND have the confidence to move on. You are not only able to gamble but to go on your own. Unless it means going forward, they do not hesitate to torch bridges.

SUPPORTERS

Happy citizens are generous contributors. They know and are reassured of the "truth" that as long as you are honest in your gifts, the more you give. We work under the premise embodied by Zig Ziglar's quotation, "You'll get what you want in life if you support a lot of people to get what they want." The only thing you can offer is not money. You can provide time, know-how, money, etc.

STRONG SELF-ESTEEM NATURE

Unique people feel that they deserve their popularity and realize that they should do anything they want to do. You know that a mistake is what you do and not who you are. I also track the early signs of poor self-esteem to help retain a good self-image. They know that self-esteem is a state of mind, and it's much more critical for them to prefer to have high self-esteem than to have low self-esteem.

QUICK TO BEHAVE

We also hear of people who have the talent or who dream of a big game, but who do little. Those who waste their whole life, believing it will never succeed. Doors, not speakers, are productive men. Until they take steps, they do not consider the situation to be excellent. You just obey it, hear the input, and change your next move. Many in their lives who accomplish nothing appear to use 'Will,' 'Can' and 'should' a lot. Those that never get what they want are too late to justify themselves and reach their next objective. I advise you to find out some realistic ways to avoid procrastination.

CONFIDENT

It is what allows us to act effectively. Like chicken and egg, confidence will enable you to accomplish your goals, making you more optimistic. A great way to trust is to remember and conquer the fear of disappointment in the past. Trust means respecting others, not judging them individually, and knowing that you still get the strongest and better the first time you do it. A mixture of confidence and integrity is a win.

GOOD READER

Many people want to learn, if not always, right. If you think that achievement is reflective and that you can achieve by thinking and behaving like a productive individual, reading will be an essential part of your everyday life. I have come to understand that it is vital for me to read books that make the most sense to you with access to more books than I can read in many lives. These are typical books that allow you to become a real authority on your passion or criticize your own restricting beliefs.

INTUITION OF TRUST

Those who excel in life have faith in their 'nice.' You do not explain why or how you acted rationally, but you knew it was the best thing to do. Successful individuals learn to use their subconscious influence by transmitting "words" from their conscious mind. This thing includes consciously visualizing the outcome in advance and then pulling in the details and evidence that would make the sub-conscious the materials for the execution of the submitted "files." Knowing how to meditate is also a perfect way for your intelligence to grow and communicate.

OPPORTUNITY TO LEARN AND WELCOME

Two people run a race and get to a massive wall that blocks their way. One individual sees the wall and tries to walk down to waste his time and wants to abandon the race before losing any more time. The other person thinks instantly about what the odds to get across the wall are. Is he/she going to mount, smash it, crawl under it? Whatever alternative you chose, you act on your decision and seek your input. No matter how you want. Good people have a positive approach, and they never hope they will learn about someone else. You integrate other people's aesthetic characteristics while at the same time, minimizing negative qualities.

ACCEPTANCE OF ONESELF

This acceptance was right to Polonius when he said: "To be true to yourself." Those who excel should not pretend that they are not anything. It allows them to share their imagination fully and not care about hiding who they are. The only way to consider one another is to respect others truly and to embrace them. You still just don't so much respect yourself because you choose to criticize others. The worst form of denial is self-rejection.

DREAM BIG

I've always got to read a wealthy person's biography but didn't have big ambitions to do it. Sir Richard Branson, Walt Disney, and Sam Walton were both huge dreams and accomplished much more than they expected. That is one of the reasons why they succeeded. You don't care about thinking big and go with it. Ask them about the visions if you want to know if someone is going to excel. They don't think big enough if they sound believable.

GENERALLY ROUNDED AND EQUILIBRATED

Those with outstanding achievements aspire to excel in every part of their lives. They lead a balanced life, become financially stable, cultivate positive relationships, improve their leadership skills, and accomplish their professional objectives. You know it won't help you improve your true potential by losing one primary field to another. You have to think about how you can pay the bill, and it is impossible to do your best to make donations.

OUTSTANDING NETWORK

Competent people understand why partnerships are critical and how they are one of the essential drivers to achieve your goals. It is also apparent to them that helping others first without receiving any benefit is the easiest way to create a secure network. Many that do not give up continuously create an extensive network very severely.

FASCINATING

The joy they have for their love and their lives is a sure indication of someone special. You are up in the morning as you know it will get you one step closer to your dream. Successful people strive to be leaders as others are drawn to their passion and become supporters to do the same.

RECOGNIZES FAULTS

You should do two things to ensure you are not useful in the future: blaming others and apologize. You give up your duties and control while you do all of these things. You are merely implying that if anything goes wrong, then you accuse other people or making arguments. You have no control, and then problems happen to you, not because of you. Good people confess that they are mistaken so that they can work on the issue and not waste a scapegoat.

ABUNDANCE MENTALITY

Successful people should not treat satisfaction or success as a minimal way to deprive someone else satisfaction and achievement because you gain happiness and prosperity for yourself. You assume that there is plenty to go around and that it's more about profit-building than the competition. It is the attribute that makes them content with the achievements of other men. This mentality frequently supports other people's confidence.

WELL PERFORMED CHARACTER

Heroes are victorious men. Think of the heroes (films, novels, real-life) that you meet. Were they not both truthful and integral? Generally, they're not charitable and frugal with others? Do they not just lookup? It is no different from being a hero who triumphs in creation.

GOOD COMPANY

As I grow up, I remember that through the business, they have a lot of knowledge you can know about anyone. Experience this idea when looking at people you meet and remembering with whom you share the most time. Some people claim that the average wage of a company is typically the five most people they get.

That is how people with conventional views prefer to stick together. It happens. When a group spends 65,000 US dollars a year, and everyone inside the company thinks it will gain 65,000 US dollars per hour, the people in the community would think it insane. However, the party of someone paying $65,000 an hour will estimate his religions in earning potential with the other person receiving $65,000 a year.

For you, what does this mean?

You are surrounded by people who live their life and pick up their values and their routines. It could mean spending less time with the outgrown men.

GOOD LISTENER

Many people want to be great writers, but not many people are willing to be good listeners. Listening to people excel in their lives because they can sense and appreciate other people's needs and spend their attention on fulfilling them. Listen carefully and ask questions, the best way to be an energetic conversationalist.

SELF-CHECKING

Good people never lose power. You don't scream or rage blindly. You have learned to control their impulses and are in a resourceful state knowingly (or subconsciously). You realize that you can't own or control what happens to other people so that you can change yourself and how you feel about it. Given how you think about it, another indicator of self-control is what you will be doing.

ALWAYS GET READY

Unique people are also set. They have Plan B and plan C, D, E, and F. They have Plan A. They rehearse the scenarios internally and imagine them visually to "think" what to do when the real situation happens.

CHOICE

People are in charge of who is right. You know you have a choice still. Their DNA, backgrounds, and circumstances do not make them victims, so they honestly do not feel the experience has decided the future. You write the story in life.

CONNECTING TO YOURSELF

Productive citizens trust each other. They don't have to be allowed to do what they want, because other people don't allow them to slow down by depending on them. You trust in yourself, and your desire to fulfill your goals, whether or not anybody assists. Ironically enough, it is precisely this kind of mindset that encourages people to support you.

AWARE OF CAPACITY

Many who are great know that effective energy management is equally critical, if not more, than time management. Knowing that rest is so essential that practice is one of the vital crucial concepts in energy management. Successful individuals know that low energy outcomes are weak, and their need for quality is breached. Sleep your path to success is one of the better ways to manage your resources.

And where do you stand?

I think that you've verified several of your skills or generated action plans to improve the skills you lack. Use the ability to cultivate one or two at a time. When the values and behaviors of a competent individual are harmonized, you are shocked by how good you are.

START WITH A VISION

Before they buy the dream, people buy into the chief. —Maxwell, John.

A collection of goals helps to picture the real essence of management. Do not merely talk about an abstract picture but describe the objective with focused clarity. Remember the end goal time and over again to make sure you are committed to the finish.

Nevertheless, it is not enough to set goals. This thing is equally necessary to execute the aim and objective. Provide the team with a straightforward, practical course. Stay patient when it's impossible to trust in you.

Neil Armstrong will not be the first man on the moon without the bold dream of John F Kennedy. Once you know it, no idea is too tall.

CHAT REGULARLY AND SIMPLY

Good leaders are almost always perfect simplifiers that can sever debate, dispute, and skepticism to give us an answer. —The correspondence from General Colin Powell is the primary connection between dream and fact. Lend the message of clear clarity and commitment at all corporate levels. The employees must understand why they work on a mission, what they can do, and where they should go. It means that they have excellent interpersonal skills, are a keen listener, and can solve problems. Efficient listening abilities are an influential leader.

DO NOT UNDERESTIMATE THE POSITIVE FORCE

Build a door if chance will not knock. – Milton Berle. – Milton Berle.

I had the opportunity a few years ago to invest in a Walt Disney leadership workshop. It was in 1928 in New York that Walt discovered that his supplier had recruited the bulk of Disney animators to launch a new studio. My best insight was this fantastic event. He lost nearly everything, including his staff, his jobs, his profits, and Oswald, Rabbit's hit hero. Then he gave his brother Roy a telegram reading, "Don't worry. Don't worry! Everything good. All right.

Optimism leads to the channeling of irrational anxiety and confusion into creativity. Skeptics will surround you as a dictator. Reject pessimism and transform constructive numbers.

ENCOURAGE AND INSPIRE

You become a leader because your acts inspire you to think more, learn more, do more, and grow more. — John Quincy Adams People build mediocre labor and get out of it quickly without the right stimuli. Some people are motivated by strength, opportunities, respect, and exciting jobs. This thing is up to you to recognize and inspire your workers with different motivational variables. You can also nourish the squad, which in effect, is a perfect source for success and commitment by taking care of them.

GREATLY WELCOME REVIEWS

Leadership and understanding each other are essential. —John F. — Kennedy. Kennedy One way to learn and develop is to embrace positive criticism gracefully. Many administrators, in particular CEOs, believe this "advised by their juniors" in their capacity is counterproductive. Your people, however, hold the key to crucial knowledge that might help you excel. Leave behind your pride and wonder what else you can do.

MANAGED BY EXAMPLE

You don't drive people to find out and tell them where to go. You proceed to this position and make a statement. —Ken Kesey
Forcibly, teaching and training are over. This thing is the foundation of future leaders through the talk. Seek to convince people not to lose time. Instead, prove your action the advantages of a clear decision. You can't afford for other people to do something you don't. You will set higher expectations and deliver more reliable performance in addition to gaining value and faith.

Thinking of your role model is the best way to proceed. What would you imitate? What are the characteristics of this person?

TAKE RESPONSIBILITY AND TAKE ACTION

A strong leader is a person who takes more than his share of credit and his share of the loan. —John Maxwell.

Don't tell anyone the blame. It is the least qualitative attribute any leader may provide. Working at the top ensures you own the dream and the decisions of the staff. Each company will have its share of slips and mistakes if they have a good range of internal controls. A great deal of bravery is required to justify mistakes and take action to correct them.

USING CONTROL TO SHIFT DRIVES

If the sea is calm, everybody will hold the helm. "Villain Cyrus."

Successful people never lose hope and temper in any situation. They are the boss of ourselves. Such people have the power to drive the ideas accordingly. As a dictator, you frequently face obstacles involving daring and different decisions. Confidently use your intuition to your benefit and authority. Progress is inevitable to establish a stable development environment.

GROW COMPOSURE

Patience and perseverance have a mystical impact when challenges vanish, and barriers dissolve – John Quincy Adams.

You recognize that a life cycle requires sprint times, followed by rest cycles. All of us are susceptible to prompt and pressurized decisions. Be cautious when excited and want fast results. Be careful. This thing refers in particular to small firms and entrepreneurs, where diligence will make or kill.

NO 'SINGLE' MANAGEMENT STYLE EXISTS

Swim with the latest in style matters; stand like a boulder in theory. —Thomas Jefferson.

How could a single way exist if there are no two people exactly in this word? Daniel Goleman researched over 3,000 mid-level executives, investigating six distinct types of leadership: order, revolutionary, associate, republican, and pacesetting. The engine behind these strategies is cognitive insight, which has a significant influence on an organization. While specific strategies have a more negative effect, they are ideal for other circumstances and individuals.

Both these cards are up for successful leaders who respond to the demands of their case. We are versatile and switch from one style to the next. To whom do you most identify? Prepare to relax and master the ones that are left behind.

CHAPTER:6 HOW TO INCREASE AN INFLUENCE & RAISE AN ADULT

WHY BECOME AN ADULT CHILDREN'S ROLE MODEL?

I remember how they became my role models when I spoke about my childhood. For, e.g., my mother settled a comfortable table, and with any holiday, she and my father would wrangle lonely stray. They encouraged me to try to be a kind hostess and something more. As I tried to combine motherhood and work, it was not easy. It took me too long to use the Wedgewood that I got for a wedding and packed it fast, that my 12-year-old child asked if the food was fresh.

I believe that any parent sees himself as a framework for the actions and beliefs of children. Yet children's worlds expand exponentially, and our impact is quickly diminished as a broader range of taste-makers have both positive and negative control—our impact declines per year. When children become adults, the sense that the sell-by date for character development has expired is quick to accept quitting the roles model business.

YOU SHOULD NEVER AVOID BEING A ROLE MODEL

The tragedy in parenting is that if you're good at it, you get killed! Your kid is off to college or the "real world" by the time you've finally discovered the fundamental realities regarding how best to discipline your child.

When you face a devastatingly complicated menu of parenting options, you'll have a specific but essential reality you can use to keep track of the wellbeing of your parenting style.

"If I'm hardworking, caring for my family, and leading a good life, my children would follow the path. See my point, are you seeing? The nature of the interaction is crucial to shaping people. On this point, there are tons of data.

However, one day, you will undergo an awkward awakening when you are as comfortable as being a good example. The purpose of my blog, like my psychologist for hundreds of parents and children, is to explain why.

LET US CONTINUE WITH WHAT I THINK IS A FUNDAMENTAL TYPE OF SUCCESS FOR PARENTS

The best hope of a healthy child is to have content + decent holidays + early schooling + children's internalization of the value system + spending Decent Time with children (QT).

Now I've purposely purchased them, and I know individual families are giving them. This is, it takes more effort and time to provide material items to the infant (it isn't a specified priority, though, it ends in this way). Some of you will GASP and say, "These men must be what horrible parents! "Well, think about this: How long is shopping or looking at the material stuff distracting you spend with your child? When you're honest, I bet more than you know.

I agree that we will spend a lot of time doing this, our kids need things. But it goes far beyond material need, and there is it they need. This thing takes me to the order I teach the hundreds of parents I served within Tucson and the entire country as an educator and clinical psychologist. How significant is my sequence?

They are helping children to adopt the framework of interest + investment of quality time with children + schooling + necessary supplies + quality holidays.

The critical task you have is to help your child internalize a set of beliefs that is their anchor on the rough seas of life. Here's the ticker: if you're not spending enough time with your kids, you probably won't internalize your value system. Any of your positive habits can be picked up, as they are genetically related to you, and science teaches us that genetics plays a part in who you are. Yet the world has a much more vital role to play. Parents do not spend enough quality time with their children. One of the most common and damaging mistakes I see parents make.

The specified quality time: we ignore our devices, our careers, our egos, and our personal needs and spend time with our kids daily, where we are talking to them more in-depth. We're laughing with them, and we're getting curious for them. We're rolling with them across the board. We should play with them in the doll room.

Of reality, we're doing within purpose what they want to do. If our five-year-old would like to ride a Ferrari to see what she can do on an open track, we may want to consider a different choice. Yet we take artistic interest in them, and we are pleased and curious about the benefits of our kids. We share their dream. Maybe we search on the internet for Ferrari's or go to the auto show for Ferrari, etc. And, we could draw photographs with this machine. It's just about us having fun QT with you. Parents will also show interest in the needs of our children and express them their dreams to be better parents. And we remain one of the fascinating people that our child knows through this QT we share.

We also internalize those ideals for which we have the strongest and dearest ties. You'll find that they are far more likely to listen and be like you by making your QT warm, entertaining, and enjoyable with your kids. You are most likely to come to you.

MOST PARENTS ARE OBLIVIOUS TO THE VALUE OF THE QT BEFORE THEIR PUBERTY

Warning! We don't want to waste too much time with you until they become a teenager. Yeah, they're going to come to you, just for cash and benefits more often. Yet you always want to see you, and when they feel pain, wounded, depressed, or confused, they will go to you for advice. The probability that these teenage years will come to you is strongly linked to how long you put in when you're younger. Your goal is to make a deep impression as a child so that regardless of how much he hates you (during such stormy times), he or she already considers you to be a person he or she cherished, respected, and admired. And think fascinating. So fascinating.

Sure, not always does your kid love you; you still have to admire you. The motivation that you will always have is profoundly tied to the degree. Which you feel you've been involved in who you are.

One of the most tragic things now that I see is that parents let their bond with their child be disrupted by technology. I noticed two teens seated at a table with their iPad at a Mother's Day diner. That was deplorable. But technology approaches and ruins the bond between the parent and the infant.

I know the parents lament when they come home from work, and I am a psychologist, therapists for babies, that they are too drained, so I sympathize with that. Nonetheless, the belief that partnerships are more relevant than something else, computers, the internet, etc. is ingrained in our family lives. One law we have in our house that whether the technology that messing with marriages, then for a long time, it will give the child a lift to help them to keep their devices from being so obsessed with them.

YOU SHOULD CONTINUE TO ASK QUESTIONS TO TEST YOUR CHILD'S HEALTH: HERE ARE QUESTIONS

Why are they saying they want you to be a part of the day if you told your boy what children want to do if they could do something for a day?

When someone told your child when it was the last time, he had QT when all external stimuli (including text) have been deleted, could they mention anything within the previous week? And in recent days? Can you list the top 5 interests/passions of your child right now? To what degree have you discussed and helped them develop and improve their bonds with them?

How did you determine how parented you were and how positive habits you wanted to adopt compared to what poor habits your parents needed to bring an end? Grandparents have the confidence to question each day, frankly. If you feel too angry, contact a source like a psychiatrist or a doctor who can help you work through that. Some specialists, such as myself, deal with emotionally dysfunctional parents or people who wish to change and develop their childhood. Just one or two meetings will make far-reaching changes!

How many routines (like meal times) do your family have to on a given day when all equipment disappears, and it is QT?

QT IS ALWAYS HARDER TO CUT OUT THAN SEEMS

A parent of five told me a day when her daughter read three books together, one of her favorite moments, and the mother then strokes her child's back before she rests. It may sound insignificant, but it's QT too. This caring mother does several things all at once: it encourages the child to learn how to read, to learn to shift quickly through a sleep period to help the child navigate the night with comfort and care. And the planet is balanced.

A FEW OF MY FAVORITE WORDS IS THAT YOU CAN'T BE A KID IF YOU WANT THEM

Some in becoming a kid may not realize that if you don't carve out QT frequently, you won't carve your kid QT for you as your child gets older. You're going to get sad when you grow older. You should carry it to the store.

Even Facebook won't make you know like your kid is prepared to take the time to come and see you from their busy life for the adult. The goal of view of the adult. Teach your child that a strong, romantic friendship with someone else is one of the most valuable qualities. If you do, you're going to stop too many of the issues. This thing would allow an enhanced choice of partnership, better decisions of friendship, and better choices of alliances. You'll know what a healthy fellowship with another entails. You'll know whether or not someone indeed does. And you gave them a basic concept of how you feel to be genuinely and compassionately associated with others.

THE EASIEST WAY TO CONNECT WITH ADULT CHILDREN AND PARENTS

Some parents of underage children have trouble believing, isn't it? Or the parent still in diapers with multiple babies, right?

It's, but – rarely.

You have no control over their life after adult children leave the family. You don't "pop" them anymore. The only chance you have is to manipulate them. When they graduated from high school, the "raising" part was mostly completed. Or only though they have a license for their car. Parenting primarily affects you when they are away from you, and when they will do what they want to do while they are gone.

This is why early catching your heart is critical to maintaining your control. Even then, sometimes it lasts and sometimes it doesn't so you can do nothing if you're there.

Your curiosity for them, your urge for support, or your feelings for them – thus often strength – does not decrease.

What will adult children's parents do, then?

Okay, I'm still very young, and I always hear about it. I got a lot of things I learned. I have even learned a couple of items from the many hours spent with adult kids' other parents – and their grandchildren. As a pastor, adult parents in our churches are an upcoming fight. I couldn't tell how much I've been seeing in adult children over the years of stress, resentment, pain, and even rage. I know a few young people who do talk, but who, by the way, that it was given to them, do not control their parents. I know that some of the parents of adult kids watching adult kids making wrong choices, so I don't know how to handle them.

Luckily, with my two adult daughters, I have a great friendship. Two of my closest friends, they are. Yet, I'm attentive. In their lives, I want to protect my power. And sometimes, I know the lines are sensitive. So, I reservedly deliver these reflections, realizing I don't know anything, but I have some "experienced" feelings. Mobiles and classrooms have made it affordable, convenient, and more immediate to exchange knowledge. Yet is it good for parents to retain a quick or continuous contact — in either mode of communication?

For parents, traditional modes of contact can be stressful. Most adult children don't respond to their mobile phones; they keep the voicemail boxes filled, so it is unlikely that you would leave a note. You will not read by recipients until you give them a warning text to read your post.

Nevertheless, as one study shows, after interaction with adult children, parental feeling varies; under various situations, it can be very uplifting or disturbing. For short, you can't get to your adult child with a mixed blessing.

WHY INTERACTION WITH ADULTS AFFECTS MOOD OF PARENTS?

The emotional best option for parents may not be to phone and fax are grown people, over the face to face contact. The study titling "The ties that bind: Midlife Parents' Everyday Experiences with Rising Children" revealed that 96% of the 247 sampled relatives with children aged over 18 talked to, written, or seen in close contact for one week, Karen Finger man from the University of Texas, Austin. There was regular interaction with a startling amount.

Yet, the scientists needed to ask interactions were influenced by the nature of the interaction between parent and infant, whether they had a significant impact on the parent's attitude and well-being.

A MULTI-REACTION BAG

'The optimistic and pessimistic everyday moods of the parents have been linked with fun and challenging encounters with grown children,' reported a study. Of the many parents who talked to their children during the study week. 88% talked on the telephone, and three-fourths were seen directly. "Almost all" subjects smiled or were discussed well.

However, over 50% had hostile encounters, including a "nervous infant" or a kid with fear about babies. Most parents had positive or negative interactions, and none had neutral interactions.

THE PERFECT PLACES TO CATCH UP WITH

The consistency of the relation between parent and child is essential; the extent and the type of communication depend on it. All three contact forms (telephone, email, in-person) were more likely to be used by parents who had more successful interactions with their adult children. Many with an overall good relationship about one and a half times wanted to see their children in person.

It is also notable that when interacting with children by telephone or text messaging, parents reported more negative relationship content. In the intimate touch parent-child in comparison, more negative partnerships were not dramatically related. One part of this research challenged the type of relationship most closely linked to parental issues. Investigators wondered if there were more parents worried about children in healthy relationships, for example, worrying about their health. The contrary has been found: "The infant of parents who had fewer supportive relationships is more likely to be traumatic.

GOOD CHATS HEAL NEGATIVE EXPERIENCES

A successful parent-infant relationship appeared to alleviate the detrimental consequences of a dysfunctional child, regardless of the adult child that triggered the original parent dysfunction on one day. The same boy or girl might be calling later that day to share a joke at work or an amusing story about how his baby sings the ABCs while asleep. The beautiful story will mitigate the trouble about the problem.

How do you talk to your adult kids? How much does this happen? Are your messages, texts, and emails ignored? Are meetings in person less disturbing than the online links?

CONTINUOUS PRAYER

Pray with adult children like nuts. For them, intercede. You don't have to remind them who you are – but I know who sometimes they would like to hear that really though they are not. Finally, motivate yourself until you continue to pray for them while you are inclined to think about them. This thing is more reliable and can be affected by one of the best forms.

SPEAK WITH RESERVATIONS

Should not express all your thoughts on how you can treat your life. It's their livelihood. In too many words, they cannot tell you, but even children in adulthood continue to live their life, much like you may like to stay in yours. You should share it on occasions, mainly when told if you think they are making a huge mistake, so if you share it, it's no noise in their lives. The irony is that when you add too much, "their" life again when they need it most, you decrease the influence of your voice.

BE A ROLE MODEL FOR THEM

Be the more experienced in the connection. It's important, right? You have more experience, and you're not expected to have more maturity? I had met parents who handle their adult children with silence when they didn't call when or work as planned. Was this the mature answer? How it plays, does it? It may be responsible for a response, but it does not encourage safety.

I know other people who use indirect coercion or place excessive pressure on their adult kids to call, to participate in other activities, or merely to respond to them in some way emotionally. Yet again, it can be the product of your skills in deception, yet it does not create a long, long-term, stable friendship that you ultimately desire for your children. (And that does not take care of it. You crave their love and wish for it).

Design the conduct you think to be that of your adult children. They are more likely than sentences to imitate actions.

KNOW THAT YOU WERE YOUNG ONCE

This thing is a secret. Recall what generation was like that. You want to learn. You've been dreaming. Perhaps you've been afraid and confused. I don't know what to do. You managed to put all of it for a few days. You understood it all not. You still have to know. You get angry occasionally at the parents. (Hopefully, you are still.) And you were made worse by those people. Recall? Attempt to understand them by recognizing you again at their age. When you can communicate for your period honestly, you will affect them more.

MAINTAIN THE DOOR OPEN

Be available to you as you put yourself at your side. When you lock the door, whether you draw sharp lines in the ground or when you make rigid guidelines about the relationship, it can be a lot easier to open the door again. (They roam even though we love Prodigal Son's tale because we love them too much!) You don't have to make them reap from you. You should set limits, in particular those that are in your house or for their more significant benefit. (This is not true love) (But remember that it's not your interests and for their excellent.) Any unnegotiable problems can occur, but let them be uncommon. You are seeking to build a long-term chance to affect them.

MOVING THEM RATHER THAN YOUR OWN LIFE

You cannot enjoy all the decisions you make. You might also think that they're wrong. Once, share your thoughts if there's an open door. I guess the easiest way to write a letter is even whenever contact is stressful. Yet again, it's not something you raise — you affect. So, they can accept your power, or they cannot. So, admire them more than you fear the choices they make in their lives, generously and unconditionally. And make sure they know that love is always unconditional. It will secure your power in the future — if not now. And in the days ahead, you should be pleased.

PROTECT THEIR HEART

Hold your heart and your life-particularly. Be mindful that, for years to come, you want the chance to think about their lives. Be here intentionally. Be careful to make decisions or do something that you can regret later on, or that will take you further. Do with your spirit – and yours as you do. Just like all those years you sought to shield your heart, you shielded your back. Ideally, you would have the opportunity to talk with their lives about their performance, disappointment, and knowledge as their power is secured as they can articulate their purpose.

And you bred them for this, recall. You have made your parents, you have made it into the world, you have taken chances, and you have brought it to yourself. They're just going to try like you did, and they're going to make mistakes as you did.

Don't fill up your mail before sending the recipient's e-mail address. How many e-mails you think were received by accident? None of me, but that's a lot of it. Don't be one of them. Don't be one of them. It could also have catastrophic consequences.

"The more you are, my easy rule. The more fruits you eat, you know, the more vegetables you consume. You know the healthy habits of everything. The more good habits you learn, the more good habits you become. (Unfortunately, that can be applied to bad habits too, so look out for yourself. It can seem all right to perpetuate a bad habit).

ATTENTION

It's all like the secret of everything. Hold your options and actions in mind. Don't be crazy for momentary or impulsive choices. There's a slight degree of spontaneity. This is fun. Not too much jumping through big decisions.

You love your brothers and sisters. And if you don't like them all the time. Once the end of the day comes, they're the ones for you. You're fortunate enough to have some good friends, but they somehow don't equate to family love. Do so until the day you leave this world, or I'll continuously haunt you.

Know that with all their hearts and souls, your parents love you. Perhaps once you have your babies, you'll understand this. This thing can sound incredible back then. After all, we didn't let you do much, and we haven't always been sweet or fun. We're still not that sweet or funny sometimes. Who thought it was one of the most challenging stuff to love you?

CHAPTER 7: WAYS TO RAISE AN ADULT

You also find the children to be self-extensions. Whether or not they are indigenous or imported, this is valid. Sometimes people say "blood denser than mud," but not necessarily enough that you can see Step-Dad's deep love for their foster daughter. You want the most for your children when it comes to parenting. That is why there is always no job worth losing the entire family life because it is a short jump to the next point. But how can you tell your kid what you have learned when you have your own business in order? A joyous and happy child is the vision of any parent. Establishing an infant is an act of conscience – no one accidentally succeeds. You may want your life to begin while trying to fulfill your goals, but how do you do it without paralyzing your children?

The iconic actor and martial artist Jackie Chan famously recommended that he give his hard-won fortune to his children as his inheritance precisely zero dollars. He claims the ultimate golden spoon is just going to hack them down in the long run – an audacious tactic. Have you ever wondered how to grow up a healthy and prosperous child? Any more, you will teach a healthy and happy kid. No more look here.

And if you chose not to do so yourself, it's real. Why do you build patterns without being a dictator in your children, so that they gain trust and achieve success?

I AM TAKING INTO ACCOUNT THE FOLLOWING OBSERVATIONS:

It's not easy to raise a kid. We always think as parents about what our children want, but never wonder what the children want. We believe that we know more than we do and therefore make correct choices. However, once we consider what they say carefully, we find that we just need to do something sometimes that children say. Every parent wants to raise children who are healthy and prosperous. Yet there's not much parental advice out there.

1. KEEP ON TOP OF IT

It may be weary, and often you find that the words go to and fro in one voice. But British researchers have found that parents with strong aspirations are more likely to have children. That grow up to be successful — and escape certain main pitfalls. 'a survey of 15.000 British girls around ten years of age, from 13-14 to 23-24 years of age, showed that those whose parents regularly had strong aspirations of their children were:

1) More likely to study at university.

2) Unlikely as teens to get pregnant.

3) Without a possibility of extended work periods.

4) Without a chance of being trapped in a dead-end, small-wage jobs.

ADMIRE THEM

Parents honor their children in two significant ways. The first comes because of their natural abilities. The second is because of their actions. For instance:

1) Lobbies for inherent skills: excellent work! You are so talented! You are so smart!

2) Lobbying effort: Excellent service! You've been living and finding out!

Low front line: thank children for their actions, not talents. You applaud them.

It is attributed to Carol Dweck, a psychology professor at Stanford University. Her dissertation focused on the teaching of the distinction between that disposition and a set disposition.

Yet when you thank me for my commitment, you encourage me to develop the muscles that you want me to build.

Consider again if you are a reasonably young parent and assume that this kind of difference is more necessary because your children are older. Only infants from 1 and 3 years of age will assess by the impact of these reward techniques.

LET THEM OUTSIDE FOR FUN

That one is easy. And it's entertaining for both children and you when the weather is good.

Consider this: all of us who work in workplaces continually told that we are murdered all day long. And then, for six or seven hours, what do we want our children to do? Sit back in the lectures. This is out of the mad maps. Science indicates that you can allow them as soon as possible to play outdoors.

"The more time children have spent their time lying down, and the less time they have spent on physical exercise, the fewer improvements they have made in reading over the two intervening years.

DO READ THEM CAREFULLY

This is particularly important when they are younger. Highly effective children's parents are those who taught their children while they were young. And the way is right, and the way to read them is incorrect. This turned out.

Only to learn is the wrong way. We were both (I plead guilty) here; occasionally, you teach your children so carefully that you're like autopilot. I may, at this stage, recite from memory the whole Ladybug Girl series of books.

But if you do, your child does participate more successfully in reading. Ask them to read book pieces. Tell them what the story would be like it. Tell them to change the pages for you if they're too young.

"If you were the baby boy, what would you do?" she wants to say. "The child can come up with another response that character can make, a different choice that character can make, even in books that you read 216 times together."

LET THEM PERFORM JOBS
It's a real item, I promise. Why do we, as young children, develop work ethics?

It's what you have: you make the meals, you mow the grass, take the garbage out, go to the house, clean our rooms — all the things children sometimes steal, and parents have to catch up for them.

"It is not just about me and what I need at this moment ... they know that I have to do the work of life, to be part of society." The downside as a parent is here now. Since asking a 9-year-old to fill it, you have always seen what the dishwasher looks like. Have you ever had to wash up after your 7-year old walked the dog with a bunch of plastic bags?

The argument is that it would be much simpler if you did yourself, especially in the early stages. The argument is: Yeah, that is not the case.

SUCCESS BECOME HAPPY

You are the world's first contact your child has and are a significant influence on him (allow me to use the men's word to identify both sexes). As Olukayode Alfred rightly said: "The first touch in a foreign country is most affected by you."

You are the first contact a child can have on the world and at home as a parent. A happier parent makes a joyful child; good children have the same thing. A successful child is likely to be affected by a successful adult. You are a tasty and healthy individual, the first step to raising a successful and happy child.

FAMILY TIME SHOULD BE MAXIMUM

You have to make time for the family alone to raise a good child. Your family wants time to express their feelings. It strengthens the family bond. Offer your family a time to feel at home, including babies. It is quicker for people to pitch ideas. You can fix challenges and raise mountains while you're with people who you're happy with – your kin. This is the basis for a healthy and happy child to grow.

FAMILY MEALS REGULARLY

There's an atmosphere that encircles meals. It's a happy glow. Make sure you have time to sit along with your mates. Make sure that you prepare the daily family meals. It's not a regular occurrence to be. During a week, there could only be three breakfasts and four meals. Cooked food is fantastic in the kitchen, and you can spend more time with your children. You can eat together as well.

CELEBRATE LITTLE ACHIEVEMENTS

A funhouse produces a glad baby. Families who celebrate their members' achievements continue to be healthier and happier. In contrast with homes where wins are not given priority, children from such homes appear to be more successful.

Promotion, decent marks, accomplishments, and other fantastic things are something you should enjoy. Just when it's the only party you can afford at this moment, you can celebrate with your family always.

PRUDENTLY SOLVES DISPUTES

You have to know that the state of your home impacts your child. Unresolved disputes never operate academically well for children from their families. Many of them have issues with their friends and men.

This generally leads to violence, alcoholism, and misuse of drugs, depression, and other social issues. Freeze it as long as possible if you have some tension in your house. Your child depends heavily on joy and achievement.

GIVE ATTENTION TO YOUR KID

The average four-year-old will be asking over 200 questions a day. Is it not that good to have an effect orally and nonverbally if the responses he or she gets were? The exchange of information between the groups involved is two-way communications.

Offer him your undivided attention while your kid is talking to you. It means having kind eyes and listening to him sincerely. You may need to lay down what you occasionally do at the moment. It makes him communicative and means that you listen carefully to him.

TEACH HOW TO MANAGE EMOTIONS

I think you need to know that any time I mention teaching, I mean – by behaving and not by words alone, introducing them to them. You would be able to concentrate more as your child is emotionally stable.

He won't get quickly carried aside or trapped in reckless decisions. The health of the body and mind is enhanced. Make sure your child understands all emotions, but not all actions, are appropriate. Empathize with your child, show for off, and appreciate the success of your child.

SENSIBLY LIMIT YOUR CHILDREN

In a law-abiding family, good children are brought up. We assign all and thugs to homes without laws or regulations that tie them on them (if we would call them apartments). The first part is: kids want to be free, but not to lose.

Children who are viewed with laissez-faire behaviors appear to become purple, and sometimes feel that parents don't matter. For the boy, that's terrible. The second part is that they should be small but not so choky.

The kid is in isolation or overstrained. It's dangerous. We appear to be too nervous when the first opportunity we get out of control. To raise a good and glad boy, set sound rules, and clarify the idea behind these rules to them. You will be caught by surprise as soon as he understands that the regulation applies.

GIVE TIME TO REST

Obesity, reduced brain function, and lower productivity are some of the effects of sleep loss. Based on the tasks carried out, there are various types of rest.

Take the time to rest for your child and regain energy. Be sure your child has ample time to get a decent night's sleep. Take the night rest to ensure that it is met with them. Limit the time of the screens and events late at night, which may disturb your sleep.

During your vacations, you can also make an afternoon snack. A peaceful mind is typically more successful, adding to a child's success and happiness.

ARRANGE PLAY TIME FOR YOUR KID

Some of the mistake's parents commit are that their children are not allowed to play. All works, no play, Jack makes a boring boy. You must encourage his child to play openly to make his child happy and successful.

Encourage him, not just video or indoor sports, to play outdoor games too. Although you can play Scrabble and other board games, you do need to ensure that he attends football or track meets. This ensures his physical and mental growth.

TV WATCHING TIME-LIMITED

Research has demonstrated, that the time spent in front of the Television and happiness have an opposite relationship. However, as in broadcast workers, there are a few exceptions.

Teens and adolescents are more likely to be anxious about that TV time. Be a good example and always restrict the exposure on television. Try to spend the day relaxing or chatting with your kids.

COURAGE YOUR CHILD TO READ

Someone of success has odd reading habits. Teach your kid yourself to read this. Per book your child reads successfully, maybe you add a bit of incentive. You can read a lot of books from your child's textbook to fiction, history, business, and work. Your child can read them.

Short stories are like a nutrient for the intellect, which stimulates thought growth and creativity. Take advantage of the right books and let your child grow into a good and healthy adult.

NOT THE END JUST FOCUS ON MEANS

Don't make the mistake of showing the results and forget about it. Make sure you show your kid how significant the outcome is. You will, therefore, encourage your child to keep up with the ideal outcome always.

This way, children gradually achieved more. Look out to consider the actions of your child even though you don't produce the intended outcome.

ENCOURAGE FORMING NEW RELATIONSHIP

Nobody will ever live alone. A partnership must be established. 'Show me your friends, and I will know who you are,' you are advised that you will decide your life with the sort of relationship you have.

Learn to develop a healthy relationship with your child. It will be to improve him and drive him to prosperity. For your child to develop friendships, you must construct an environment a spot to check your company with others.

YOUR KID WOULD BE ALTRUDIST

Productive people believe like their lives have a sense of self-worth – value for others. One way to do that is to teach altruism to your kids. Inspire a charitable boy. The period is one of the things for which they might be generous. Especially when they give of themselves freely, compassionate children are happier.

TEACH THEM TO SERVE OTHERS

Favor and support self-service orders. Enable your child to volunteer when the opportunities in the family, school, and community are available. Do not forget to carry your kid with you while you volunteer.

Give him space to support you, not only does it develop your abilities, but also increase your confidence. Encourage your child either as an adult or as a team or a family to support and benefit others.

YELLING IS PROHIBITED

There is virtually no excuse for raising your voice against a child who knows his right from wrong. Screaming also causes more problems than it can fix, so why do you scream first. Your pre-teen can lose confidence and become vulnerable to shouting. Screaming is a symptom of an abusive home, and children from these homes are more likely to doubt themselves and feel distressed. You can always do so when teaching your child emotional balance.

If you are on the verge of tears, stop or leave the room until you are calm. Unless you should think about circumstances and come to a decision, do not yell to your recognized kid. You want a courageous, healthy, and successful kid, and you want to feel their frustration and let him know why you chose.

TEACH YOUR KID TO FORGIVE OTHERS

People who do not forgive are less likely to be satisfied. Unforgiven hinders real and sincere joy apart from alienating the human. Without redemption, it is unlikely for anyone to have a second chance. Don't take rancor and also don't let your kid carry rancor. Just make sure that you agree with the good ones by changing the incorrect ones. Forgiveness is typically fulfilled and less likely to experience anxiety and depression.

PROMOTE POSITIVE THINKING

Performance, happiness, and positivity go together. The truth is, no one with a good outlook will be happy. Have a good perspective, and let it be seen in you by your kids. Don't whine or take a minute to make a huge deal. Instead, maintain a good outlook and speak positively. Tell your kid the dark cloud's silver lining. They are hopeful and reflect on the bright side of events in this way.

ARRANGE GOOD CHILD MENTORS

As long as you see your boy, he still wants other hands to support him. In all but him, you can't be that. Help him and find a coach and support him. Trusted adults increase their odds of success in a child's life. Your coach can be a trusted friend, tutor, or a trustworthy member of the family.

ACCEPT YOUR CHILD'S MISTAKES

Luckily, in your life, your child can make no errors. Luckily, it's the ethic that your child wants to help develop. Which do you think is your child's healthiest way to grow? It's never going to be off and never have to make plan B.

And do you want them to benefit from and be open to errors? Growing up, being more educated, and making that experience as value? You would eventually restrict your independence if you were to choose the first choice. It is necessary to encourage your child to recognize errors. Provided they are still introduced, and never included in their narrative as the main statement. Overall, if they make a mistake, they will never lose, even if they forfeit. The healthiest thing you can tell them would be to smash the faults.

MOTIVATE THEM TO TRYING

The best musician, swimmer, or athlete, does not require your boy. At part-time jobs, they don't have to be the best. Yeah, at the age of 10, they don't have to train to write correctly. In the IFBB tournaments, they don't have to become Mr. Olympia or a successful star

But you have to do anything you're involved in and do your hardest. If you let them still realize this, the undue strain will be reduced, and they will be motivated to keep moving and succeed. They will not be burdened. Just safe should it be. It will also inspire you to invest in your hobbies and passions, for instance, if you choose to check out these top 15 latest NAMM 2019 items.

ALLOW THEM TO DO WHAT THEY WANT

Another thing is to follow in your footsteps, so to watch them do so can be very embarrassing. They will never be pressured to do so, though. You've got to create your reputation. We are enthusiastic about the future when you grant them permission to do so, which would be perfect if they want to adopt the motion. Otherwise, this is perfect too. It all depends on the point of view. You will undoubtedly grow a happy child first and a good second with these tips. Ironically, this improves the likelihood of achievement in your career.

Let me tell you that your child has a significant impact. Yet I'm not trying to do that because shaping is not something you should do now and not later. I also named the first argument, "The kid affects" You're already manipulating them, even though you're not sure of it. He knows from you through the actions of speaking to sleeping, how you communicate with people (including the child). That is why certain children are going to act like their parents.

THINGS CHILDREN WANT FROM PARENTS

1. Showing is more comfortable than asking me by seeing you when I am a kid. Give me a role model.
2. Send me kisses and embraces, loving me. With such, you can't trick me.
3. Child and strong discipline my brain continues to grow, and I learn gradually. Yet, I want to know if you

teach me with wisdom and compassion.
4. Be still here for me, irrespective. Be my place of refuge.
5. Don't just talk to me.
6. Talk to me. Listen to myself occasionally, without judgment or copying, and I want to be understood.
7. Don't equate me to other children endlessly.
8. I'm going to practice a lot outdoors.
9. Give me a nutritious and cheap food. Give me milk.
10. Confidence, I let myself settle about issues not linked to protection or fitness. Without slipping, I could not learn to walk. By taking bad choices, I can't try to make right decisions.
11. The support means so much to us.

CHAPTER 8: HOW TO RAISE BOYS

As a mother of boys, you also understand their inherent distinctions from your children. Yet what do you do for these differences? Why do you discipline your children so that they are open, responsible men? According to

Dr. James Dobson, author of Bringing up Boys, "the job is to turn [our] boys from untimely and transient boys into decent men, faithful and obedient to us, and secure in their patriotism.

We should also make the environment more child-friendly and particularly kindergarten. Most boys at the age of five (and some girls too) aren't able to sit down – their brain development is potentially dangerous. So, they are not able to know rote or have to read and write. They have to. They do much better in countries where children begin school at six or seven. Many youngsters, but particularly those active boys who have a good need for it, play and be busy.

This is only the beginning. The boyhood stages are not open to children. Another of which is the "full fours," which put puberty hormones well ahead as luteinizing hormones invade their bodies.

Four-year-old parents note elevated movement rates, rumbling, and disruption. It's a relief to know that it's not nonsense. (Although it is worth getting to the bottom of an abrupt shift in actions if there is anything bad). Yet it is prevalent for young boys (and some girls) to break out with excitement, and our job is to work out how they would do it – like they would have to do if we had a sheepdog in the room.

You should go up and wander about and have fun with lots of places. And help with learning how to put the brakes on a little soft but simple. When we make a child feel guilty because he is a child, we trigger insecurity about being loved, which usually comes out as frustration and a poor man's beginning. You should set boundaries and remind him to rest; please do it kindly.

Researchers in the Royal Children's Hospital, in a long-term survey of 1.200 children entering their twenties, found only last year another stage of infancy, called adrenarche. Adrenarche arrives at the age of 8 or 9. There is an increase in the number of hormones named adrenal hormones. I name this "emotional eight" because it's usefully presented. Your son is more likely to get frustrated or nervous or run abroad and is not generally his own. He's as puzzled as you are. Adrenarche is the initial puberty stirrings, but visible symptoms do not appear for three to four years.

More boys than girls end up bigger or heavier. Now that girls and women are so special, it is essential to teach them never to strike, injure, or insult or even rude. The emotional period mostly coincides with puberty, which mainly occurs two years longer than with kids, and when they hit full height and are entirely fertile (thankfully) is around fourteen. After 16 or 17, kids cannot grow in height or sophistication.

However, most boys are taller or heavier than girls, and consequently better than their friends. And it's utterly important to warn girls or women, from their mothers or sisters, never to beat them or even hurt them. Together, fathers and mother's ought to reiterate that message, stay with them, and recognize a decent man and wait and never go for anything else. Again, not strong or rough, just friendly, but clear crystal. To become a decent one, a child must know just what it entails (and, of course, see it done by the people with which he grows up).

Train your son when he is young to live the right way, and he can learn the best way to act and treat himself as he is older as he has been taught during his youth. We may not always be doing it "right" as parents, but each day we will try to do what we think to understand best about them.

THERE ARE SEVEN IMPORTANT PRINCIPLES FOR RAISING BOYS:

SHOULD KNOW ABOUT VALUES

How you teach your son influences your beliefs. Find the principles as the central foundation for all parental activities.

In any region, our values affect our parenting. Therefore, it is really important to learn about our beliefs. For starters, if you want to treat others as you wish, that will influence your child's teaching to respect others. Yet that would also influence how you train your child to take care of others because you first respect yourself, and anyone else is secondary.

A child encouraged to respect others as they do themselves is more likely to share their toys with their peers, and they realize they want to share them in this situation. Their peers are more eager to share their toys. A kid who is encouraged to think about himself first is less likely to share, as he has discovered that it is more important to get the toy than to share the toy because it is more valuable than others.

Learn your principles and your heart as you teach your child in essence. The following tips are helpful only if your child is trained to be a good, moral citizen with positive values. A structure of ethical principles and a sense of justice must govern their actions. It is the foundation for all the other abilities.

GIVE WAY TO THEIR POWER

Understand why your boys are more violent and thrilling than your girls are. Channel it into something positive instead of trying to suck their resources.

KNOW HOW TO REBOUND FROM DISAPPOINTMENT

Downfall's a life feature. Whether a man does not manage to excel will affect his capacity in the long term. When a man feels exhausted and cannot pick up and start again after a loss, he will never be through. As men are encouraged to gather and try again during their youth, they learn how to get out of defeat.

It is a good lesson to tell your son to try again after defeat. It can be achieved by highlighting the commitment and not the result.

For starters, you would drop several times before your child learns his talent if you teach your son to ride a bike. You inspire them to get up and do something over and again. Do not emphasize the outcome, which runs on a two-wheel bike alone. Rather, thank them as they have worked hard and stood up and tried it again. They will finally learn to cycle successfully after an ample attempt. You should certainly compliment them as they have the potential to learn, but once again, make sure to emphasize their hard work and perseverance until they have succeeded.

Time, commitment, and energy are required to succeed. The easiest way for your child to develop a mindset that produces results is to increase concern over the result.

When you rely on the result, for example, winning a game, when you have a failure, you feel defeated.

We are now likely to see where we could change if they can go through the game and appreciate their hard work and their positive efforts. It's going to make them stand up and start again, so they don't look like an utter disaster. You can see the benefit of their good work and a mentality that can start again, and that can be changed.

CARE FOR THEIR ESSENCE

Understand that in this world, many scary things can harm the heart of your people. Dobson recommends that "the threats must be aggressively treated, exposure to public abuse minimized and symptoms of distress, kidnapping or lethargy are detected."

TRY TO KEEP THEM NEAR TO YOU

Hold your sons in close touch. Maintain free contact, direction, and discipline by devotion. Kids tend to be with their kin. I like both mom and dad for quality time and quantity.

Many conditions are not sustainable, in particular considering the rise in single motherhood levels. Studies have shown that single mothers raise boys well, provided they have a good role model for children. The next best thing if the dad cannot be in the picture is a decent father, who will affect the child's life positively.

According to the National Economics Editorial, single motherhood in the U.S. is around 40%. When contrast with children in typical families in which both a mother and rear father, children with single mothers have significantly lower moral test expectations and are more violent.

However, for single mothers, all hope is not lost. Our everyday life's work found that having the presence of a parent or grandmother in a child's life would help the child boost his or her educational results. They are less likely to be arrested, less likely to experience substance addiction, and may experience greater confidence and good self-esteem. This helps young people tremendously. They are not to be taken lightly. Our children need good male role models, and if possible, a father in their lives, to help them grow and succeed.

When a dad isn't in the picture, instead, the void can be filled by a brother, uncle, or family member. Good role models are important as they form the way life can be carried out. Kids deserve to spend time with a parent, or a strong male role figure, to figure and tutor, and to encourage them to be decent guys.

BE A ROLE MODEL FOR THEM

Provide good role models for your children. When your dad's not at home, try sharing time with a close family member or relative.

GIVE YOUR TIME PROPERLY

Give your children plenty of time with each other. You may need to change your timetable, but give your children time and content. People think that a boy can become vulnerable with a hug or love. This just doesn't happen. We show them how to kiss and "I love you" is behavior that makes them better boyfriends, wives, mothers, and role models as adults. It also gives you tremendous benefits, including physical well-being, lowered anxiety, enhanced coordination, increased gladness, and decreased health-line tension.

Some therapists prescribe a minimum of 12 snacks a day for progress, and others suggest as many snacks as we can and offer better outcomes on a regular basis.

Everything wants attention and affection. Hugging is a primary means for parents to have a happy, supportive every day for our children. Depending on their home experiences, our children tend to be affectionate. If you grew up in a family that has never earned a cuddle, you would possibly find it uncomfortable as an adult. Inform her that affection is good and let her take advantage of those kisses every day. Use it as a habit to embrace your son regularly and say, 'I love you.' The benefits are, therefore, important to you.

SUPPORT THEIR NEEDS

"Counteract the impact of man-bashing in our society by the reinforcement of the manhood and the importance of a boy as a human."

Kids will have visions. Dreamless life is a dreamless life. Don't pinch your hopes by crushing them before they can attempt to follow them.

Your child may want as an adult, for instance, to be a professional footballer. Hope and vision were theirs. They're 14, and that's their desire to survive now. Many parents have decided to make those visions seem impossible. The prospects of becoming a professional athlete like a footballer will be slim, but they should not be trying. They must learn over time that they are truly strong enough to leap to the next stage by their involvement in the sport.

That's why having your child be well-rounded is vital. As the old saying goes, you cannot put all the eggs in a single basket. Rather, the value of other activities should be learned, and the school will work hard, and you never know whether the accident will actually keep you out of a sport. And if it sounds like one in a million shots a kid follows their dreams, they are given important life lessons. You know how to work hard, and you figure out what it takes to be the best thing you dream of.

Nothing positive happens easily in practice. If this is their dream, then let them do it (not to sell your house to finance the rocket development project). Enable them to earn the rocket fuel. We will see what it takes to get there like that.

If you don't reach that goal, it's all right, too. It is interesting to hear what they have learned along the way. We heard about teamwork, physical fitness, planning, and dedication, for example, as a football player. It wasn't anything at all. They will never become a pro soccer player, but over time, they may discover the truth.

A parent wants no truth to break illusions. Enable children to hope and to dream, for this is what makes them do their hardest to make every effort.

The opportunities to work hard even with disappointment are good things to learn from experience. Don't discourage them from chasing a vision because they are scared that they will embarrass themselves. Failure and the desire to get up after a defeat ensures that they are powerful guys.

A RELIGION NURTURE

Make the spiritual growth of your children your first priority in parental education by encouraging them to establish their relationship with God.

TRAIN TO PLAY A STRONG PERSON

A good sport is a key learning capability. In practice, we can't compete. Everyone will ultimately fail. Parents should teach this ability to their young children.

For starters, when you play a board game, and your brother loses, you should not sulk but congratulate your brother. When you have played, have you told them verbally "friendliness, good game." Starting young is a healthy idea. When they've been able to meet other champions along the road, it will make it more enjoyable to be a good athlete as a teen or an adult. Stanford Children's Health described healthy sports as:

Good sport can seem impossible to decide, but its defining characteristics include being able to win, value one's rivals, and lose with grace.

TO BUILD A STRONG ETHICS JOB

Do not do everything for them! Do not do everything for them. Try to train your kids to work with a strong work ethic. Although mum does it for them every day, they won't learn to make their bunk. Via everyday practice, they learn accountability and positive professional ethics.

It should begin at a young age. Once the kid is three years old, he can assist with the necessary household activities like recycling garbage, gathering toys, feeding animals, and washing. You may not do the best job at all, but you begin to educate you when you are young. Provide them frequently with critical life and family knowledge through education. This allows you to build a strong ethic at work. You will grow up and know that you can throw out the garbage until it is complete, as you have done it for years before you reach maturity.

Don't presume why other household tasks belong to boys and others to girls. Teach all girls and boys all their skills through activities. Sons must be taught cooking, sweeping, and washing. What would do things for them as they leave home and go to college or their first job? You must learn these skills to do better for yourself.

This makes them both a great, preferred 9partner and husband. No woman wants to marry a man who can't do household work. You may fault your parents for not educating you, but if you do not know how to commit to homework, it will not help you get a better partner.

Having a successful girlfriend, husband, and wife means having able to do things like washing and cooking, and having washing, heating, and all the homework. This is not a healthy way of educating others for themselves, or train them for any partnership in the future, to ask others to do so when their moms did as they grew up. When you would ever like to stay alone, outside your home, teach them sound work ethics, it ends with household duties.

TEACH STRONG QUALITIES IN CONVERSATION

Communication skills are essential for any child's relationships and professions to be productive. The foundations for human contact are communication skills. If they find it difficult to connect, relationships and career goals can become more challenging to achieve. Livestrong.com notes that technology is a big reason for the lack of effective listening skills for many youngsters. In an environment of pervasive email and instant messaging, their face-to-face encounters are impaired. So much time is spent outside of positive face-to-face experiences. The very first step in establishing effective communication skills is to limit your child's exposure to technology and resources. Speak to your child every day, and chat is useful in developing positive communication skills.

If you already have a teen who has trouble acquiring strong qualities in speech. Not too late. Not too late. We can also learn these skills, but during our lives, we can still develop more vital communication skills. One approach to teens is by sports. Good contact. Strong listening ability can be learned by chatting, form these skills, and open-ended questions for those of those with younger people.

This involves laughing, complimenting, posing questions, and responding kindly to justify their guidance. This method of speech, both verbal and nonverbal, is an excellent means of educating children and can help children build friendships both now and in the future.

FREQUENTLY INDULGE IN POLITICAL AND MANNER LECTURES

It is not a one-time lesson to teach your son good ways. It's a daily childhood lesson. Take time every day in your house to use and apply proper etiquette and politeness. It is how you can help your son become a respectful man. It means you can show them how to eat socially from the moment they prepare to sit at a dining table. We should try to eat with their mouths closed on the dining table, and use the best silverware, no cocks on the table. If you don't learn to exercise those things at home, you won't develop the things via natural means.

In relationships, courtesy is significant, but also on the front of the job. Study.com demonstrates that you should train for career advancement and referral letters in an appropriate style. For example, if you tell your son that he can be respectful and accommodating to others, even though they are not especially good to him, that will help him learn how to interact in the future with rough co-workers. In his life, your son still is going to have rough men. Finding good ways to treat them is important to his life's progress.

ENABLE HIM TO GROW HIS CHILD'S HEART AND DESIRE FOR SUPPORT

To our girls, compassion is something that we all will like. Your generosity to others will affect their environment. Not just your relationship with your future wife, but also your future children, your coworkers, and your friends.

Teaching our children to be kind makes them change the environment. Some realistic ways to make your child kind are available:

- Model compassion
- Teach the principle that you treat someone as you expect them to love
- Take them on volunteer service to and serve someone (when you are compassionate in your heart and positive in mind)

- Teach them to express words of appreciation and sincere gratitude towards others
- Lead them never to be a tyrant
- Teach them to treat people with respect, because it does make them behave in the right manner, it is nice
- Model appreciation
- Teach children to be thankful for their lives and situations

CREATING SKILLS INSTILLING PEER OPPOSITION DETERMINATION

Parental pressure is actual. Pair competition is a reality. This starts when young and does not end in adulthood. We must teach our babies, even though their peers seek to bring pressure on them in other decisions, to make good and stand up for these decisions.

Skills You Need explains ways in which we should teach our children to peer resistance. It involves training them first on how to recognize their correct judgment in these conditions of social pressure, how to speak up for their opinions and beliefs, and eventually to show them how to express their stance assertively.

You can help them to practice their defense of themselves and their decisions by playing scenarios with your child. You may play a part, for example, where your child receives nice medicines. Practice them first by asking you that they want to say 'no' to drugs because they have to trust in the decision. Help them then to find belief in their belief so that they have a firm basis for their decision. When they don't think they want to, their only excuse might not be adequate because it is their closest friend who guarantees the closest they will ever meet. Enable them to realize their beliefs and why they say no to drugs, or whatever the scenario you watch.

Then advise them to respond no strongly. In that case, for example, it may be because they are learning ways to express it in their terms which is relaxed but firm, such as "no, I'm not taking drugs, and I'm not going to lose my right to attend college for the failure of a drug check or being caught doing the drugs."

Teach your child by justifying their positive choices to avoid social pressure. If you know any of his buddies had a disabled kid on the playground, but he was sticking up for the boy, then pick up his wife! Let him think that it is smart decision-making to do things better and not to do as his friends did.

We need to learn where they are in critical problems to be peer-resistant. The next tip is also quite necessary.

EXPLAIN TO THEM THE IMPORTANCE OF HEALTHY LIVES

If they learn right from wrong, they can't make good life decisions for your kids. This lesson ends in the building. If you want to improve your son, encourage him to make positive decisions for his future, including no drugs, alcohol, underage drinking, and pornography because it is seen as extraordinarily addictive and counteractive to healthy growth. Which are not the only forms of drug avoidance vices of parents?

While alcohol and drugs seem to be the most prevalent stimulants in adolescents, illnesses such as videogames, gambling, sexuality, shopping, or the Internet cause other addictions, any excess which affects the ability to work on a daily basis regularly should be dealt with. Some of these problems should be avoided, for example, to discourage game abuse and not to grant your sons available free time. Have set daily gambling time limits and technology access. Have your son interested in fun gaming events so that he doesn't just concentrate every day on his time in the game. Support him to pursue these other things, and he wants hobbies and passions beyond gaming.

Discuss with your child the choices they make for their lives and how their choices will impact their future. For starters, a teen might feel that smoking marijuana often isn't essential. One may be unaware of the zero tolerance of the narcotics program, even the marijuana, at the institution they plan to attend. Often, the dangers and drawbacks of smoking pots for teenagers may not be understood. Address the main problems and even the minor ones. Before taking bad calls, have the tough talks.

A parent gives a list of supportive ways in which parents can assist their children in making wise decisions. Help them see the consequences of their choices, even minor ones. You should not believe your child's science experiment, for example. We are the only ones who will not get an exhibit on the day of the science fair. You didn't call for your help. It was probably because of suggesting to you that they had a job to be completed before the day before. Their choices have consequences, and guardians must encourage their children to understand that their actions and preferences have a personal impact.

If a mother feels sorry for her son because her science experiment isn't finished, so she whips something for him when he sleeps the night before it leaves, then the son learns because his mother will save him as things get rough. He won't feel the regret that he hasn't had a job and can't attend the technology trade fair. Since mom fixes problems, he won't get a poor score.

Over the long term, it doesn't help him. He must undergo these shortcomings in order to grasp the consequences of his acts and decisions. If a project does not finish, it will lead to failure, and in the specified amount of time, he made the conscious decision not to do the job.

HONESTY IS THE BEST POLICY

Adult dishonest and deceiving people have an evil heart. When you want to make your son a man of honor, so from a young age, they have to understand that honesty is incredibly necessary. Below are a few ways that your child should be frank.

1) Honesty Template.

2) Do not say white lies because kids still cannot distinguish between small lies and significant lies. Do not fib at all, because you are their only truth-telling role model.

3) Promote sincerity: When you believe you should be disciplined for telling the truth, you won't be told.

4) Giving your child a chance, without pushing him, to tell the truth.

5) Should not commit children's lying to make your life simpler. Of starters, it makes you a thief to convince them that the park is closed and you can't go there today. Do not even lie to your kid for a better or more obedient life. Be blunt. For example, when you don't have time to take them to the park, then you can't go to the park today, but two days later you'll take them there and as you've agreed.

6) On your word, please be good. If you say something, do it. This makes you cheat because you don't follow through.

7) Don't be accusatory because you ask your child to know the truth about a case. When you are, for example, suspecting that a lamp hit your son in your living room, don't run to him shouting: "I think you've hit a lamp, best tell me what you're doing right now." Forcing an honest answer out of coercion doesn't encourage him to be honest. This tells only when the truth gets him into trouble, to cover the facts.

8) When you confess to lying, think to the victims and about how their mistakes and relations have hurt. Enable them to see that relationships are detrimental and deception.

9) Praise your child for having said the truth, particularly when it may be hard to tell the truth.

SUPPORT HIM FIGURE OUT HIS STRENGTHS AND INTERESTS

When you're not serious about what you are doing, it is impossible to excel. For our children, that's the same thing. We have to discover what our children are passionate about in life if we want to succeed. The easiest way to attain achievement and joy is to learn what they are good at, their talent, and where their interests intersect.

Parents must be careful to identify the skills and natural capabilities of their sons. Then, if your son loves doing anything, give them a chance to discover and develop their ability into an exercise. If you see your child getting a strong synchronization of hand and eye with a goal, you may want to engage him in a soccer season, for example, and you love tossing a goal in your backyard at night. This will become a hobby if he retains a skill and loves the sport.

Learning to develop a skill with enthusiastic determination is a major skill that allows them to excel in their lives. It's difficult to be excited when you work hard if you're never passionate about anything. They'll discover their willingness to search deeply and work hard where they find love. This allows us in the long term to establish positive work ethics. As people, it would make them glade.

You, as a mom, should help your child experience things and experiences that make him passionate about his life at a young age, so that he or she can find ways and opportunities to improve his / her talents to make this desire for a cause work.

TEACH HEALTHY HABITS FOR RISING

People with inadequate treatment can have trouble with relationships and work. If they are interviewed in a warped costume, poor breath, and body scent, they advise the interviewing person that the role is not sufficiently necessary to try to look and smell good.

It's an ability that all boys should be taught is essential to dress nice and clean. You will know how to use iron and how to fit clothing correctly. Boys should know what proper grooming and cleaning practices mean from an early age as well.

Parents need to teach their kids how to comb their hair every day, how to trim their nails, shower daily, clean their teeth, change clothes, and frequently shower or bathe. Many boys are avoiding proper grooming and taking care of their bodies during periods. It is where parents will participate and set specific grooming standards. For example, if your son fails to shower and you rule to shower every other day, and it was a week now, then you will forfeit all social rights and technology, for instance, before they shower.

In training them, you know how to look after your bodies. Good grooming practices can be a routine that starts as soon as you can clean your own teeth. We don't know how osmosis can do these things. We need to be shown how proper grooming and personal care feel.

Both conditions can be resolved and avoided in certain ways, including stinky shoes, body order, and greasy hair. Decent people must understand their sons how to have cleanliness and safe habits.

IMPOSE AN AMBITION FOR EDUCATION AND KNOWLEDGE

Your son needs to be trained if you like a mechanic, a hairdresser, or a neurosurgeon. Wisdom is power. The day we want to stop rising is the day we no longer have to know anything else, which is why, as a life-long endeavor, we will instill in our children that we are never terminated with knowledge and learning. Give your son always the joy and enjoyment of education and learning. Enable him to figure out the books will motivate him to do everything he likes.

Of starters, he may want Lacrosse's sport. He doesn't know much about the sport, so he looked at a game and decided to check it out and join a squad maybe. He should brace himself if he is able to learn about the sport.

The exercise of athletics is extremely important, but it is also useful to understand the rules and how to use the equipment correctly and what exercises make it a better player. Tracking a book at the Lacrosse Library will be of benefit to him before he goes on the field. In order to be good at it, he has to be able to master the sport.

Nevertheless, schools and books alone do not need to know. It's a product of life and mentorship. The urge to do something positive can only go as far as possible. We must always be able to learn and to develop by integrating accumulated expertise and experience.

TELL ABOUT LIMITS AND HOW TO RESPECT OTHERS

Boys are going to be men, never a valid reason for misconduct. Good behavior expectancy starts in the region. Children must be trained to honor others, especially elders and women, in particular. We will carry this conviction with them into their matriculations, jobs, and adult life because they are educated at home that women are inferior. When boys are told that women are equal to men, they tend to honor them.

Would that mean they have the same skills? Sorry, not that. Women can't give birth to children anymore. But that doesn't make us inferior with varying skills, and it just affects us. Encourage men as boys to value women's strengths and values to support girls and children. In the future, it will also teach you to be a better friend, a better husband, an attraction for the same sex. If it is taught that women are less than men or that women do not need to be respected, it will probably be said and followed up by those thoughts. The driving force behind our actions is our emotions and convictions. Our actions transform into our life.

Within our culture, domestic abuse and sexual harassment are real and pervasive issues. Of much larger weight, the majority of criminals are men and women. Domestic Shelters is a domestic abuse awareness agency. They say 85 percent of victims of domestic abuse are women. People from childhood must be taught that abuse, in particular against women, is irrational. You must always be told that 'no' means 'no.' If a woman or a girl doesn't say anything about physical improvement, she should stop.

If children are taught to support young people, and it is taken to heart, it avoids abuse against women. But it should've been an ongoing dialogue during the youth and adolescent years to speak about how to handle women would not be a one-time discussion.

It is also important to provide good behavioral models and relationships. If a husband abuses his wife, sons who watch teach and learn this pattern of abuse. Tell your sons never hit a lady, but in the fitness of anger, you strike your mother. Your acts are going to talk louder than you think.

HAVE THEM DO ROUTINE PHYSICAL EXERCISE

It's not easy to raise girls. By the moment they're little children, they will be hard and tough with lots of potentials. I do that myself because I learn how to handle or regulate my twins for more regular strength. I realize they need lots of room and opportunities for physical fitness because most kids are physiologically so. Attempting to reduce resources because they expect substantial academic success is like hungering and anticipating a child to overeat.

In order to excel in school, children need more physical exercise. The game time in school is just not enough during the recess. The study has found that children require more physical activity than in leaves. It ensures that it is vital to run outdoors and play games, to get their aggression out before and after training. For long stretches, they were not forced to sit at the desks but would sit at school all day long. The answer is to make them work after school and before school if they have to sit down on a bench for a long time.

Kids lack physical exercise and are better likely to concentrate and pursue higher education every day and in reasonable periods of time. If they are not able to use their physical resources, they may have issues such as loss of attention, decreased academic success, difficulties reading, depression, anxiety, and frustration. Boys will be allowed out every day, several hours a day, and their physical strength.

GUIDE FOR RAISED BOYS FROM AGE TO ADULTHOOD

Most children exhibit different growth patterns, including in the womb. Their brains are growing weaker as they continue to develop testosterone in just a few months. So, the disparity continues – in certain facets of brain growth at five years of age, many guys are up to 20 months behind people. It's not only that but boys too different in size. Umbrian cord blood screening at the birth reveals that some babies are elevated and others low in testosterone. And high-testosterone boys find reading and communicating even more difficult. The general probability of children becoming trouble readers is three times higher than the trouble of students. And these are mainly high-testosterone babies.

Today, "girls are girls" is the last thing we would like to hear because they indeed are the worst of cop-outs. This means that we will say, "Yes, let us start reading this boy, telling him stories, reading books on bed and talking with him while we are on our day and listening to him." Don't dive him before a Television or a phone. The planet does not need people to fight buffalo again, but every child and every man must be in a position to talk. We will help our children grow up and get along with the boys.

The moment you looked into the eyes of your infant son, you realized that all your potential hope lies in your actions. Can you help him become a responsible, loving, positive man? Every mother wonders how she does in the raising of her child. Yet you would still be the kind of guy you want your son to be if you follow the advice given below.

THE CHILDHOOD OF THE BABY

STOP STEREOTYPING SEXUALITY

'Young kids expect the world to be as straightforward as possible, making it easier for them to perceive the world by placing people in a pink or blue box,' but it is impossible to undo the mindset after it is created.

Instead, stop first teaching gender roles. Provide a range of toys and games, even if healthy for children. Provide books and films featuring female stereotypes as well as gender roles such as male nurses and women's athletes.

Be always mindful that you share the duties with your mates. You are taking turns to see what you do and how you deal with different relationships with your employer doing so-called female and male household work. The long-term payback for fighting gender discrimination. "Studies indicate that people with fewer sexual expectations record happy marriages and intimate relationships more optimistic."

TELL YOUR BOY ABOUT BOUNDARIES

Throughout this point, you don't need to go physically, but it is essential to let your son know at the earliest possible moment that he can decide, when and how, who should access his body?

This ensures that before kissing or touching anyone, including grandmother, must be granted permission. Don't push it if it refuses. (Sometimes it is nice to give a hug, handshake or high-five, or wave choice, but, again, to all three its's appropriate to say no.) And teach other people the same rights to him — without consent, he is not permitted to contact anyone or their property.

SCHOOL GOING BOYS
IMPEDE THE FEELING OF DOMINANCE

For one study, about 40 percent of boys for fourth grade became more intellectual than girls. They are promoting mixed-gender partnerships to avoid this line of thought. "The more you allow children to spend time in touch with girls and see them as individuals, the more likely it becomes for them to stereotype the entire group, or think boys are more successful," So this should not rely solely on gender. Teach him to view people concerning race, age, ethnicity, cultural-economic status, or sexual preference.

ENCOURAGE THEIR EMOTIONS
Never say "big boys don't complain" or "you behave like a child," but that kind of talking can potentially be harmful in addition to reinforcing gender roles. "The energy from an angry does not decrease or go away if boys cut off from genuinely expressing hurt feelings. It can lead to misbehavior and twitch how a boy thinks about himself and life

in general," is non-profit that advocates social equity, men with traditional social, like mental concealment, are more likely to be distressed, suicidal thinking and depression. It is, therefore, essential to listen to your son and let him communicate his emotions.

If parents are trying to develop a relationship with their son under which he can reach them as collaborators. They can in, themselves from pressures that otherwise they will be forced to isolate him from their true selves, so they can help avoid the influence of peer culture — in the case of youth, of brotherhood.

MIDDLE SCHOOL BOYS
RAISE THEM TO MAKE HEALTHY INTERACTIONS

Data reveals that at least once a year after high school, nearly 90% of girls are sexually assaulted. The years at high school are a perfect time to warn your son that inappropriate remarks, jokes, or actions [to girls or boys] are never acceptable or unsuitable. Think about opportunities to communicate and keep your attention to find out what a good relationship feels.

Tell your kids to honor the option of the parent, regardless of the answer. "Ask him if the person's not involved, instead of asking why, he can respond, 'thank you for letting me know' - or attempt to modify the answer,"

The way to explain how your son deals with crushes is to illustrate how a solid friendship looks. Any of the things that you and your wife would like to highlight our shared love, commitment, and energy in the relationship, empathy, humility, and sympathy, and apologies for mistakes is very valuable. A research released in the Youth and Adolescence Review last year showed that young people living in a supportive family environment are more likely to overcome conflicts and less at risk for interpersonal conflict than young adults.

DOCILE ACTIONS OF "TOUGH MAN"

Social norms will sadly make adolescents feel strict, defensive, or even violent. "I know that a lot of the boys would think they have to be rough or strong, but there is another way to be a boy or a guy," your son says. "I don't know." You talk, instead, about sharing examples like older boys or people of your own family who respect or are sensitive and care for construction dispute resolution, or icons or other public officials, you trust pattern those habits."

Reduce your son's aggression and remind him that while rage and resentment are normal emotions, he cannot show them in ways that harm or physically threaten people. Support him to find reasonable ways to handle these feelings.

Gender-based discrimination is another problem that is associated with the so-called rough position of men. Women that are not super dominant don't show themselves verbally or assertively, or women that don't comment about boys get mocked because other girls label them derogatory slurs. Speak to your son and support him in finding ways to handle if he's at the edge. Call it out if your son allows the taunting. Remind him that there are many ways to be a human, and mocking or harassing a child isn't all right.

BOYS OF HIGH SCHOOL
BE EXPRESS ABOUT ACCEPTANCE

You no longer have to discuss questions of consent for high-school youth. They are determining what is called sexual assault, how to ask for approval, and how drugs and alcohol can affect a person's decision and consent. When older boys go to school with younger children, make sure that you have the correct age of consent in your country and period of partnership discrepancies.

STAY CONNECTED

The same recommendation applies because these children are teenagers, even because parents are encouraged to spend extra one-on-one time with their young children. "Go and lie down beside your son and play whatever he does, whether it's a match or a computer game." Boys also continue to use the time deliberately. "You can unload pressures, challenges, and deceptions and share details about your inner world," says Martin. Maintaining a one-on-one relationship allows you to continue to assist him in handling the challenging issues as he reaches manhood.

COLLEGE GOING BOYS
GIVE HELPING HAND TO THEM

A solid, quiet man and the bad guy on the big screen the appeal, but the good guys are those in real life who have the right way of coping with their emotions. "Some characteristics we stereotypically assume are repressive — stocked and in charge, not expressing how you feel."

The study indicates that parents are telling their daughters to feel like they are more often than children, and when girls get hurt, they get support from their parents rather than from their boys. "They are tired, and you are not and bad. The outcome? Most kids turn into mentally insecure guys who can't relate well — fill in or out — which makes it impossible for them to bond with other people.

OPEN-TALKING

Don't come in with questions if your son is grumpy after classes. "Tell them plainly, 'Looks like you're angry. I'm just here to help,'" Then bring it up later: there is something terrible at school I'm concerned. If he sends you a little (School is annoying), he will express his feelings. The odds are that he'll wake up, that's how much homework my teacher gives me. Again, affirm your emotions, but persuade more this time: you have a lot to do at home. For tonight, what have you? "Your son will know you're by his side so that you won't be reading, and he can be confident communicating more," he explained.

PROVIDE HELP IN ANY SITUATION

It's one thing to have boys open up to feel, to make them realize that while bad feelings can hang on, they don't last. "Children, rather than feeling, tend to focus on the issue." "To tell your child the feelings — pain, sorrow, rage, anxiety — will not always go away easily is one of the parents' responsibility, and that is all right. He'll finally start to sound better."

TEACH YOUR CHILD RESPONSIVENESS

If kids understand how people feel, so they make better friends and happier husbands and dads in the future. "Empathy is a powerful cognitive ability that makes you feel good for people and prevents you from doing bad things," he said. "It's one of your son's strongest pillars." Research suggests, though, that moms will cut off their jobs. Students at the college today are 40 percent less empathic than 20 years earlier, according to analysts. The researchers suggest two possible factors are violent video games that bog children through the suffering of others, and social networks overflowing with children with imaginary "people."

PLAY WITH YOUR BOY

Motivate your boy to choose his shoes by providing examples of what he wants, such as athletics. When, for instance, he's watching a baseball match, join him on his sofa and say, "The starter seems to be under tremendous pressure." Where are you supposed to be on the mound? "It only takes a few seconds, so you encourage your son to look at the emotions of others and put himself in their stead," "If you do that consistently over the years, you will become someone who can cope emotionally well."

TELL HIM TO STUDY NOVELS

People are reading fiction scores higher for empathy assessments than non-fiction. How does this happen? Researchers are theorizing about the portions of the intellect that we use to understand the fictional personalities that we use to understand the genuine emotions of people. And the higher our capacity to comprehend the others using certain portions of our brain.

ENHANCE HIS SELF-SENSE

You are talking of personalities that you respect. The odds are essential: a good dose of self-esteem is a common trait. This doesn't mean a guy is greedy because he feels suitable for himself. He feels trustworthy, professional, and dignified, just what you want for your family.

DON'T PROMOTE WRONG ACTIVITIES

Saying that your son can't live up to you are the best kid in the world or that you are the greatest basketball player ever. "Look instead at his strengths," he says. Young children feel happier and satisfied because they are rewarded for the things they perform (You have worked hard) and complete it (Good job), and they are more able to tackle obstacles than when I am proud of you when you get the general kudos.

DO NOT MARK HIM

Don't say the boys will never be boys or use specific terms to condemn the behavior of your son or suggest his acts are not monitored. "The signals that children receive from parents play a critical role in improving their self-esteem," he says. "This hurts his credibility because your son knows the words he hits." Necessarily, he'll continue to accept what those sentences say — that kids are troublemakers.

TEACH TO RESPECT OTHERS

"A young boy who grows up listening to sources of authority, upholding laws and engaging knows the fundamentals of respecting others," When he is a child, he will be second nature in this respectful manner.

SET RULES AND REGULATIONS

If your son uses inappropriate words or loses a key or a similar breach, if your son violates a statute, enforce consequences. "The children admire people who keep their foot to the flames," she said. "When you coddle your son without seeing any repercussions, he will become over time demotivated, lazy and unscrupulous."

SET A GOOD EXAMPLE FOR YOUR BOY

In the life of your family, handle with respect other people such as teachers, coaches, and parents of his peers. Insist he's doing the same thing. If there is a disagreement, perhaps between your son and the teacher, approach the situation gracefully. Don't go with your son instantly. "Hear the story from all sides, and even though your child is right, tell him that a teacher's grossness is never appropriate," he says. Then say: I'm going to talk to your instructor to see if this can be fixed. I want your instructor to tell me if anything like this happens again. "You should show your son the ability to fix problems while respecting others,"

SHOW YOUR LOVE AND AFFECTION

Once he was young, his son enjoyed your hugs and kisses. It is common for children of this age to start withdrawing from their parents. Yet note, people who give love have grown up to find means of expressing it to your son — even if he does not want you to be like him.

SET A TIME TABLE

Use your time wisely while your son refuses. When you want to kiss him in front of his friends, he might be humiliated, but the quick choice when he goes to bed, or a brief hug when he feels sad, would let him know that you care without crowding. "The kids like and want the mother's loving presence, even though they don't always demonstrate it," she said. "Being affectionate men, boys will feel this physical responsiveness."

FATHER'S RESPONSIBILITY

Dad has a distinct edge over Mom when it comes to parenting boys: he knows where the kid comes from because of his race. "Surely a mother can support a son, but a father will teach him what it means, and that's important," he said.

Sounds too simple, but for a son, it's essential to have a parent who spends time with him, "Warren said. Boys get a message that dad loves me, likes my company, and is there any time I need him, that's what gives them a sense of confidence and shows what good fathers do.

I handle people. Nice treat women. One way a boy knows how to communicate with women is by looking at his brother. "If the dad engages with women and his wife, in particular, he should be willing, especially during an argument, to admit that he is wrong, apologize, talk, and behave respectfully."

Get fit. Get comfortable. Studies show that many fathers share with their children the kind of aggressive wresting and hard living that allows boys to restrain their physical urges and to manage their emotions. "Furthermore, a dad who embraces and kisses his son profoundly declares his intimate presence."

CHAPTER 9: BREAK FREE OF THE OVERPARENTING TRAP & PREPARE KIDS FOR SUCCESS

Currently, many parents refuse to give their children free reception while they are kids to play alone outdoors or on the playground.

They create adults who struggle to protect themselves. In the process, they create.

On the other side, some parents go to the lengths that they have their children's schoolwork just to make sure their little kids excel. Julie suggests that students are practically treated as a regular activity to do jobs that their parents do while their teachers appear otherwise.

"Yes, of course, closeness, affection, love, frequent communication between parent and offspring, that's all good. Who among us wouldn't wish for a closer relationship with our parents?"

You have to avoid cutting their meat anywhere if you want your child to be independent at 18 years. But when are you done meat cutting? When do you avoid searching for both ways when crossing the street? When are you encouraging them to talk to strangers?

This omnipresent over-implication means that the children become adults in chronology while remaining stunted, dependent on their parents not only to lift their lives slowly, but also on lovely, light, and ethereal dreams.

The best thing is—not just the pride of charting the course in others. The morality slip-ups in overhauling their schoolwork, the brutality of being a relentless crutch, the damage that comes from turning love into performance—the worst parts are this secret message that we give to children: – 'I don't think you should. The best part is this cryptic message, which we offer to children, we over help them so that they are not weak, but since we do too much, they are degraded.

In this life, you're not strong enough; that's the message.

You're never going to be.

You're still going to need me.

Some creators – count me here – are aware that we are still taking incentives for children to build the types of skills and values that developed in the earliest days of their lives. As they run smartphones and participate in social media, they have encountered intense academics long before formal schooling. The real issue is that forcing our children too hard to "advance" and "complete." We decrease the fundamentals of learning, which encourages children to become doers — people who can handle what will be an unpredictable future and who are preparing to identify, achieve, and secure their dream of success. They don't have to remove all conventional aspects of growing up now, but we should guarantee that the foundational moments children do not get rid of this.

CHILDREN WILL DISCOVER THE PLANET

Children will spend a lot of time engaging, chatting, and playing with adults by their hands. Kids need to expose themselves to stimuli to interact with the environment, sometimes like a Children's Museum, where discovery without limits, however, welcomed, is not just perfect. So much programmed play – and time spent with the app – reduce the simple learning in unstructured sports. So the focus on "academics" early in childhood goes against decades of study into how the brain evolves (whether it is a recession, pretends, playing school) at the cost of playing.

LEARNING WITH INNOVATIONS

Children are solvers of fundamental problems. We test theories about cause and effect and understand what is more about trial and error. These skills can be promoted or quashed by adults. Children require freedom to perform free, unstructured events. Drawing pictures, using construction blocks, molding clay, and every other ability for a child to work without guidance and feedback help the children explore their creative selves. Parents will facilitate this cycle by having opportunities with clear resources to unstructured opportunities and by promoting and supporting the excitement of learning and the pleasure of drawing beyond the lines.

CHILDREN TODAY BENEFIT FROM OPTIMISM

People learn how to deal and function with approaches, which are maybe not panaceas, but resilience. Parents may empower children to think about their problems – whether it is learning to drive a bike without training wheels, the challenging school class, a friend's dilemma – and help them discuss what can be done and determine the next steps for progress.

CHILDREN ARE OPPORTUNITY HUNTER

Children do not learn to behave in the cover of the bubble — but neither should they be irresponsible. Instead of relying on "risk-taking," teaching children to pursue opportunities to learn how to do so while handling the possible downsides (to learning from them), people should understand the advantages of challenging themselves. It may be "hand-off, but eyes on," if a child tries to climb a tree a little high. Not just athletic exercise, it's not. Make sure that a kid has a confident hand-raising in class even though she doesn't know the solution.

Teach a child, it's all right to try playing at school, also though they are a little shy while they are on stage. Celebrate commitment and prosperity instead of "major gains."

CHILDREN SHOULD TAKE FILTHY JOBS

How do children perform tasks? Children should not only be able to pitch in age-appropriate ways but recognize that you cannot trust someone else to do all the dirty jobs. Let children play their part in family activities and learn about working with others to do what they need, without having to do things they are not equipped to do alone. Make them know that the world is not about you, and those who continue to do their grunting jobs are becoming productive men.

SOCIAL SKILLS ARE MANDATORY

We continue to work on forecasting success as an adult (personal and professional) by learning how to get along with other children early in life. Children must know how to handle disputes instead of stumping and shouting proactively. Working together is a skill that is nurtured through childhood, and it will inspire parents to take turns to work together as a team that encourages them to supports a mission. Communication is important-it pays off later on in other respects to speak to children and to improve their communication skills at all ages.

KIDS SHOULD HELP OTHERS

Evidence shows that children – including girls – become potential helpers when they are given a chance. When you spill it, see if your child can pick it up and leave it. They just need a thank you in return. Some research shows that supporting a child as a "healthy friend" fosters a feeling of caring for others. Explicate how we will all consider means of helping those in need, and model empathy and consideration. The ideas for raising a Can-do Child were recommended to contribute to "lasting outcomes." The laptops and piano lessons would not be omitted. Make sure that you give your kid ample time to develop all of the skills at home they will use to support them as they leave their nests.

WAYS TO AVOID OVERPARENTING

One of the most robust but most lucrative occupations on the planet is to be a father. Responsibility for another's survival may appear terrifying or intimidating, and it may exhaust you. Overpaid children frequently make their own choices or live alone in hardship. By helping your child, growing confidence and resilience, fixing challenges, you can prevent that.

Excessive parenthood. That's what we all want. Why will the loop be interrupted? Learn about four measures to avoid being over-friendly and offer your children the best opportunities to be positive, healthy, and prosperous.

In the first two-part show, we find out that flying, helicoptering, and micromanagement are another term ignoring. It is termed over parenting when parents do what they should and can do for their babies. It's over-parenting when you try to correct or discourage errors of your children.

We have looked at two (more or less) explanations that most of us do this: the quest for college and the fear of dangerous and self-harming behaviors.

HOW IS YOUR CHILD AFFECTED BY THE OVERPARENTING?

The fundamental concern is that children will commit errors and mistakes that are irreparable. It's called tragic, imaginative, and future-oriented rather than peacefully solving the problem. The kids use the phrase, "I don't think you can handle anything yourself, so I'm going to have to do something for you" as adults do not overprotect. Finally, the kids continue to accept that, yet another reasonable justification for avoiding over parenting.

This message and conviction paralyze our children from partnerships to schools, from activities to work. You slowly stop talking about yourself and stop solving problems. Why worry when Dad knows and shows you the right way to do it? You know that you don't have to be sorry for yourself. And if Mama can't bear it to do it for you? Why pick your filthy clothes up from the ground? What happens when your parents try to lessen the results or transfer the blame to own an issue at school?

Another consequence is that they are avoiding harm. We take no positive risks: a course in AP which may be tested to receive a B rather than an A, and seeks to act that they do not excellently, including filling the dishwasher, as it is not achieved to the satisfaction of a parent. You refuse any options because they may be the "fake" ones.

If you have ever found that, particularly with your kids, when things aren't perfect, your body's reaction is to do more, not less? You will raise your voice instead of dropping it if you don't care. If they struggle with the hard, instead of being quiet or giving only a few suggestions, you leap in with tons of ideas. In reality, though, a smoother voice would attract their focus more efficiently, and proposing less of your suggestions would inspire you to formulate all your strategies.

There is an apparent belief in our society that when our children struggle, they need more focus, more energy, more effort, and more compassion. Lately, Johnny looks a bit daydreamy, perhaps his parents need more attention. Each semester, Jessie doesn't do well enough in classes, so she wants teachers and parents to concentrate on something. Or Emma seems to have no self-esteem, so maybe she wants more attention, appreciation, and acceptance.

AVOID DEFEAT, SPECULATION AND EXCESS SHARING

Perhaps that applies to specific children and individual guardians, but it's not valid much of the time. It is also an excellent way to hinder our children from providing one of these things. And if we act out of love in this manner, we will create the exact opposite result. Instead of self-reliance, we unconsciously encouraged dependency. Kids become hooked. So we parents often get our satisfaction by feeling supportive so crucial for our children by over-doing. Yet they eventually know impotence instead of toughness.

OUR CHILDREN'S TOLERANCE

We also learn that it is essential to meet the desires and feelings of others to be a successful parent, spouse, or mate. Yeah, that's significant, but only to a certain degree.

When the reaction is more:

Was it better than fewer now, then? Some of the examples are there.

1) Do more about yourself and your kid less. In this situation, it is a more compassionate and conscientious approach to take for a

mom to do less empathizing and "meeting their needs" and less emphasis on her.

2) Less concern about satisfying the needs of the children and more encouraging them to take responsibility for themselves. Think less of the children's emotions and more about making them act in the best possible way. For example, "I'm no longer going to learn, and you can get the missed homework books — you have to figure out what is right tomorrow or do it." "You do not want to confess to your cousin that you're sorry, but I hold you responsible for doing the right thing."

3) Talk less about buying and grumbling and more about controlling and governing themselves. "I know you dislike your jobs, so I want them to be done before I ask you to do them. You may be sad, but please don't find a way to drag anyone down if you're unsatisfied.

Always be with your children in the way they need you, but otherwise, step away from them. And learn to appreciate the gap.

When professors, attorneys, and relatives tell you that your children appear to need more from you — attention, patience, energy, compassion, compassion — stop thinking hard. Should they do? Will you ignore them? If so, you can, of course, do better than you can. Yet they get more than enough from you in the possible case. It is also safer for if you cut to make legs impossible to find. Letting go will first make you feel wobbly, but you're going to find your heavy legs standing with practice and time.

CHAPTER 10: WHAT WOULD YOU DO TO AVOID BEING OVER-PARENT?

1) You should admit that you have learned the most of your life from 'failures' and deceptions. Recall why these aren't deadly. Offer your child the gifts of deceit and mistake.

2) Take a deep breath and ask yourself, "Whose is the problem? Either your child is wrong, or you want to step in to avoid one? "If this is (and sometimes is) your child's question, step back. Let him handle it if it is not a matter of health or welfare. He will know how he can repair himself or take responsibility for the consequences. He will discover who he is. When he wants to be there, you should be on the sidelines.

3) Grant your kids an acceptable age for home management duties. You must know that life is more than just grades and the road to college. It needs all family members to run their house and home smoothly, and they must gain useful abilities to live alone.

4) Most options aren't 'forever.' The possibilities of today can be traded tomorrow for another chance. Let the children know that they still have opportunities while

waiting for them to take steps and achieve their goals.

SIGNS THAT YOU ARE THE CHILD'S OVERPARENT

Overparenting corresponds to the efforts of a parent to micro-manage the life of their infant. Stubbornly circling the infant to make wise choices, to shield them from any physical or mental distress, and to discourage them from owning up to the effects of their actions, are some of the over-protective parent's moral priorities.

The inability of a parent to control their distress is typically the product of over-parenting because they cannot accept watching their child hurt, lose, or making mistakes. Parents frequently feel ashamed of punishment and fail to enforce the effects of punishment on their children. Continued hyper-vigilance and overindulgence may have significant effects, for example, stunting the growth of an infant and making an infant excessively dependent.

BELOW ARE THE MOTTLED SYMPTOMS OF THE CHILD'S OVER-PARENTHOOD:

YOU'RE GOING THROUGH SMALL POWER STRUGGLES

Historical power struggles may mean that you are too picky or too challenging. You could discourage her from gaining the independence she would need if you argue with a 5-year-old about eating enough food, or if you clash with your 15-year-old over how she styles her hair.

YOU START TO MAKE YOUR CHILD'S PREFERENCES

Often, there's the "only approach" or the "correct way" to do it, so that will contribute to your child's micro-management. You are over-parenting because you can't let your kid try new possibilities, for instance, to wear clothes not appropriate for him or to place a bath in the roof while playing in his dollhouse.

YOU CAN NOT BEAR TO SEE THE LOSS OF YOUR CHILD

No one wants to see their child lose, so they won't benefit from their failures if you run in and save the children if they have difficulties. Whenever they have trouble finding their homework or interfere with the first hint of a question on a play date, your child does not improve question-solving skills if you can give them the correct solution.

Kids often have to feel defeat on their own. Recovering from disappointment allows kids to figure out if they can do it better in the future.

YOU'RE CONCERNED ABOUT OTHER PARENTS' ISSUES

If you are the only person who is always worried about your six years old, who is playing on the playground's monkey bars? But you do not bear the thought of a 13-year-old who crosses the street with friends, so it may be enticing to believe that it is because you're more compassionate than the other adults. Yet consider the risk of over-parenting before drawing the inference. You could manipulate them to their full capacity if you don't treat your child like an intelligent, capable person.

YOU DISAGREE OVER HOW YOUR CHILD IS HANDLED WITH ADULTS

You could be over-parenting because you regularly debate their rules with parents, coaches, daycare providers, and other guardians about how the infant is treated. Irresponsible parents also phone teachers to suggest a better grade for their child or forbid Grandma from encouraging children to eat sugar.

Trying to micro-management is not as safe as other people often abuse your kids. In different settings, children benefit from learning various rules.

YOU ARE UNABLE TO RECOGNIZE ACCEPTABLE AGES

Overpricing is always the product of excessively high aspirations. For starters, a parent may engage a child in hundreds of activities and may also handle free time for a child to make sure she is still thriving.

Sometimes, unacceptable outcomes arise because parents have too low aspirations.

Mothers who do not believe their child should act individually will do anything – including their homework – because they don't know for their kids.

YOU DON'T OFFER MANY DUTIES TO YOUR CHILD

Unnecessary treatment is also like an excessive indulgence. You won't develop life skills if you don't delegate jobs, or if you don't want them to be autonomous. It will only be a long time if your kid is spared from liability.

It's not safe to discipline your child so that you don't have any fear. The independence for your child to be a kid is vital. Overparenting will discourage your child from going through a rich and full childhood to train for a more mature adult.

YOUR BABY DRESSING

Put your hand up if the kid's clothes already get gathered up, encourage them to put on, and assist them with zips, buttons, socks, and shoes. Culpable?

Your child will be able to dress up by three years of age, and though he needs assistance by buttons before he smoothers his motor skills. Allow your child to select his or her outfit instead of choosing what your child is going to wear. When he gets older, give him a little more flexibility before he's fully confident.

My child's fashion choices we don't always agree with, but we want to note that his clothes are a means of self-expression. Although his clothes are clean and respectable (even though he doesn't like it), let him wear whatever he wants.

CONCLUSION

I hope that the people would emulate the great learning displayed by this presentation.

Exploring children's books: words and images, this free course has demonstrated the illustrations in children's books are not mere immature items but are always considered to be unchallengeable. Readers may use nuanced cultural awareness to make sense of them. Many childhood illustration critics point out that the pictures themselves are complex and imaginative, as well as the number of diverse ways in which they blend visuals with words for stories. In certain instances, photographs and materials in children's books are not merely by-products; they are essential to the story growth.

COPYRIGHTS

© **Copyright 2020 By Freddie Cress –**

All rights reserved

This book

HOW TO RAISE HIGHLY SUCCESSFUL PEOPLE: Prepare your Kids for Success! How to Increase your Influence and Raise a Boy, Break Free of the Overparenting Trap and Learn How Successful People Lead!

By Freddie Cress

This document aims to provide precise and reliable details on this subject and the problem under discussion.

The product is marketed on the assumption that no officially approved bookkeeping or publishing house provides other available funds.

Where a legal or qualified guide is required, a person must have the right to participate in the field.

A statement of principle, which is a subcommittee of the American Bar Association, a committee of publishers and Association is approved. A copy, reproduction, or distribution of parts of this text, in electronic or written form, is not permitted.

The recording of this Document is strictly prohibited, and any retention of this text is only with the written permission of the publisher and all Liberties authorized.

The information provided here is correct and reliable, as any lack of attention or other means resulting from the misuse or use of the procedures, procedures, or instructions contained therein is the total, and absolute obligation of the user addressed.

The author is not obliged, directly or indirectly, to assume civil or civil liability for any restoration, damage, or loss resulting from the data collected here. The respective authors retain all copyrights not kept by the publisher.

The information contained herein is solely and universally available for information purposes. The data is presented without a warranty or promise of any kind.

The trademarks used are without approval, and the patent is issued without the trademark owner's permission or protection.

The logos and labels in this book are the property of the owners themselves and are not associated with this text.

CPSIA information can be obtained
at www.ICGtesting.com
Printed in the USA
BVHW030930260822
645585BV00017B/452

9 781804 316863